VIKINGS OF THE WEST

The Expansion of Norway
in the Early Middle Ages

VIKINGS OF THE WEST
The Expansion of Norway
in the Early Middle Ages

BY

PER SVEAAS ANDERSEN

© Per Sveaas Andersen 1971
Second edition 1985
ISBN 82-518-2079-0

Aase Grafiske A.S, Sandnes

PREFACE

This little book aims at presenting the Viking expansion in and from Norway, as seen through the eyes both of medieval chroniclers and sagamen and of present-day archaeologists and historians.

Thanks are due to Dr. T.K. Derry for valuable assistance with the language and with various points concerning early British history.

Grefsen,
April 1971   Per Sveaas Andersen

PREFACE TO THE SECOND EDITION

The contents of the new edition of the book remain essentially the same. A few minor emendations have been made, and the list of additional reading (p. 100) has been revised.

Disen, January 1985

Per Sveaas Andersen

CONTENTS

I. The Viking era and its historical sources 9
II. Norsemen abroad and Norsemen at home: the picture given by archaeology 22
III. The Viking and his way of life 36
    The Viking warrior 36
    The farmer 44
    The trader 53
    At the king's court 56
    At the local assembly or *thing* 62
IV. Norsemen in western Europe and the North Atlantic region 68
    The British Isles 69
    The Frankish Empire: Normandy 77
    The Isles and Lands of the North Atlantic 78
V. The Norwegian background in its Scandinavian and European context 86
VI. Epilogue 98
    List of additional reading 100
    Index 102

LIST OF MAPS

Al-Idrisi's world map of 1154 12
Scandinavian place-names in England 15
Scandinavian *-staðir* and *-setr* names in Scotland 16
Norway of the Viking age 29
Kufic coin hoards in Trøndelag 32
Principal trading routes of the Vikings — main commodities 69
Norse settlement in Cumberland 76
The discovery of America 82
The distribution og *-land* and *-setr* place-names in Norway 89
Europe in the Viking age 101

I. THE VIKING ERA AND ITS HISTORICAL SOURCES

The common picture of the barbarian Vikings, who earned their fame by harrying raids and conquests, was formed partly by contemporary European monastic chroniclers, partly by modern historians who were chiefly interested in Viking political activity in western Europe. These historians more or less tended to ignore the importance of other factors and primarily of trade as motive forces in the Viking movement.

Let us take as our starting point the statement with which a leading Swedish historian concluded a lecture on Viking Scandinavia and Europe:*) The Viking period has "neither economic nor political parallels in the history of the North. The economic and political developments of the time are closely related and cannot be isolated: The Vikings who terrified the Western world came from a land where Oriental silver was common. — This then is the background of the Viking expeditions to the West which culminated in large-scale enterprises and conquests, and not the conditions of an impoverished Northern society, expanded to the bursting point by over-population". The Swedish historian here propounds a thesis which has gained ground among modern historians, to the effect that Scandinavia, profiting by circumstances chiefly created by the Arabic expansion and conquests in the Mediterranean area, reached a central position in international trade during the 9th century. From the profits of this trade the adventurous chieftains of Scandinavia financed their expeditions against western Europe. It is a fascinating theory, owing much of its popularity to a modern conception of the economic structure of early medieval society.

However, the Swedish historian's general thesis of the years between 800 and 1050 as an era of unbounded expansion of

*) Professor Sture Bolin's inaugural lecture given at Lund University in February 1939.

northern Europe is undoubtedly tenable. The expansive spirit of the Scandinavians caused movements and changes in many fields, and the most conspicuous of these movements was the Viking invasion of near and distant parts of Europe. But we receive a completely wrong impression of the Viking expansion if we consider it only as pirate raids and acts of terrorism. It was at the same time a series of large-scale ventures to control international trade and of migrations and settlements in distant lands and islands. It was a period when Scandinavian art and craftsmanship reached a new peak of splendour. It was during these centuries that the impact of Christian Europe made itself more strongly felt than ever before. Denmark and Norway were christianized, and the seed of the new faith was widely sown in Sweden. In the Viking era the three peoples of Scandinavia were unified into kingdoms and started their development toward modern national states. Thus the Viking centuries are not only the time when Scandinavian warriors invaded and harried western Europe, Scandinavian explorers found and settled in Iceland, Greenland, and "Vinland", Scandinavian or "Rus" traders penetrated eastern Europe along its mighty rivers,—it is also a time of tremendous political, economic, social and cultural growth at home. It is a main task for the historian to examine the causes and effects of this expansion, and it is a matter of some curiosity for the layman to see how it all came about.

It has been common to term the early Middle Ages the Dark Ages. The phrase has been coined, partly to mark the intellectual darkness of the time, partly to describe a period in which few contemporary sources throw light on historical development. The problem for the student of the Viking centuries, however, is not the lack of contemporary sources, but the abundance of such material and above all its heterogeneous character. Literary sources, runic inscriptions, personal and place-names, archaeological material, all give us a vivid picture of the Scandinavians in peace and war and for the first time bring them out of the darkness of history and into the focus of European events. Whereas the literary sources and the runic inscriptions are mostly concerned with the martial and burial activities and

Page of the Anglo-Saxon Chronicle, describing the battle between Harold Godwinson and Harald Hardrade at Stamford Bridge on 25 September 1066. It was the last Viking battle to be fought in western Europe. (Manuscript E, The Peterborough Chronicle, Bodleian MS. Laud 636, Oxford; Early English Manuscripts in Facsimile IV, ed. D. Whitelock, Copenhagen 1954, p. 114.)

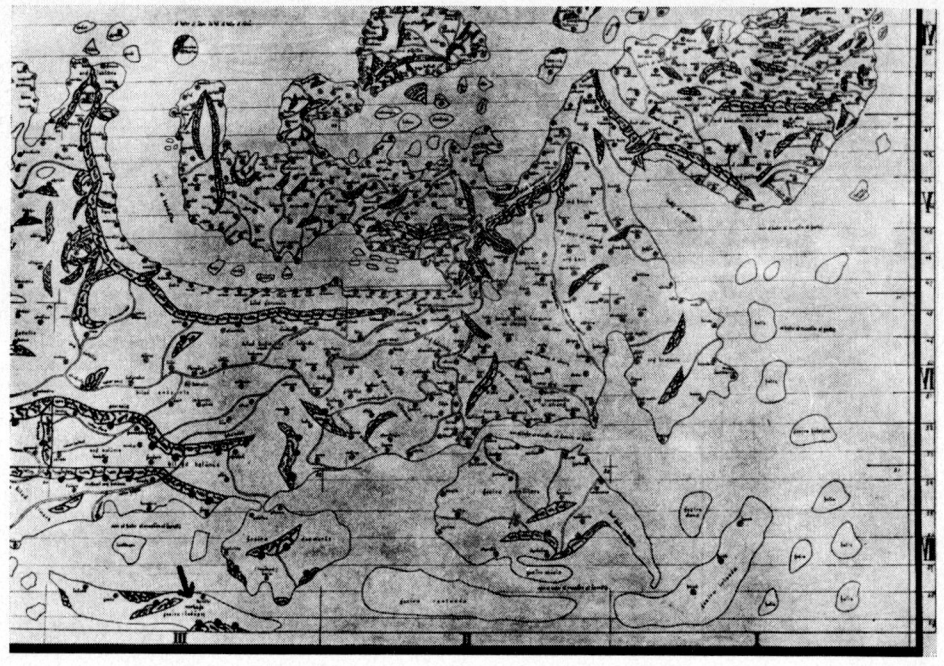

Western Europe according to al-Idrisi's world map of 1154. North is at the bottom, south at the top, west at the right, and east at the left of the map. Norway (Norbaga) is the island marked by an arrow at bottom left. (Reproduced from K. Miller, Mappae Arabicae, vol. I no. 2 plate IV.)

distant expeditions of the Vikings, place- and personal names can tell us about the expansion of settlement both at home and overseas, while archaeology has revealed to us a rich material culture under constant change and in interplay with European cultural trends.

Two of three main groups of *contemporary literary sources* are of non-Scandinavian provenance and reflect quite different attitudes to the Vikings. Whereas the Frankish, Anglo-Saxon, and Irish annalists are preoccupied with the raids, atrocities, and destructions of the *Normans* or *Danes,* the Moslem historical and geographical writers, commenting on *the Rus,* the barbarians of the North, more or less take an attitude which foreshadows that of modern social anthropologists, pointing out especially the Rus preoccupation with trade.

Tenth-century runic cross by Gaut at Kirk Michael, Isle of Man, Inscription: 'Mailbrikti, son of Aþakan smith, erected this cross for his...soul, but Gaut made this [cross] and all others in the Isle of Man.' (Copyright The Manx Museum, Douglas, Isle of Man.)

The Alstad runic stone from Toten, southeastern Norway, with inscriptions from the 10th and 11th centuries. Inscription no. 1: 'Jorunn erected this stone after..., who owned her [was married to her], and had it taken from Ringerike, from Ulvöy,...' Inscription no. 2: 'Engle erected this stone after Thorald, his son, who found death in Vitaholm —between Vitaholm and Gardar' (somewhere in the Baltic region of present-day Russia). (Universitetets Oldsaksamling, Oslo.)

The only Scandinavian literary sources (apart from the runic inscriptions) which with some justification can be considered as contemporary, are *the skaldic poems*. Although they are not preserved in manuscript from the Viking age, they are valued rather highly because of their literary form. The poems of the skalds are looked upon as fossils capable of great resistance to change, owing to the rigid principles of composition to which the skald had to adhere. As regards subject-matter the skaldic poems, however, are rather limited in scope, dealing mostly, to quote the words of Snorre Sturlason, with "the feats and battles" of the chiefs. Skaldic poetry gives expression to the heroic taste of the Viking aristocracy.

A valuable source of information about Scandinavian life and activity in the Viking centuries is provided by *runic inscriptions*. They are to be found partly in Scandinavia, partly in the Scandinavian settlements in western and eastern Europe, and partly in the wake of Viking expeditions along the rivers and coasts of the Continent. A great number of them have been carved on stone monuments along with most elaborate decorations. Such rune stones are to be found from eastern Sweden to the Isle of Man. Another important group of inscriptions are carved on loose objects (e.g. swords and wooden pins). Many of them survive only in fragmentary form, and most of them are quite short, mentioning the names of the carver, the owner of the object or the names of the person to whom the inscription is dedicated, and of the erector of the monument. The inscriptions nevertheless permit the historian to draw important conclusions as to the language and culture of the Northmen and very occasionally give information of historical importance. A flash of historical drama is preserved on the Galteland stone, southern Norway, stating that "Arnstein erected this stone for Bjor, his son. He found his death in Godwin's army when Knut [i.e. Canute the Great] went to England". Whereas this inscription seems to substantiate the general impression of clerical writers about Viking activity, another stone from northwestern Norway gives revealing information about the consequences of Viking contact with southern Europe: "Þorir and Halvarþr erected this stone for Ulv . . .. Twelve winters Christianity had

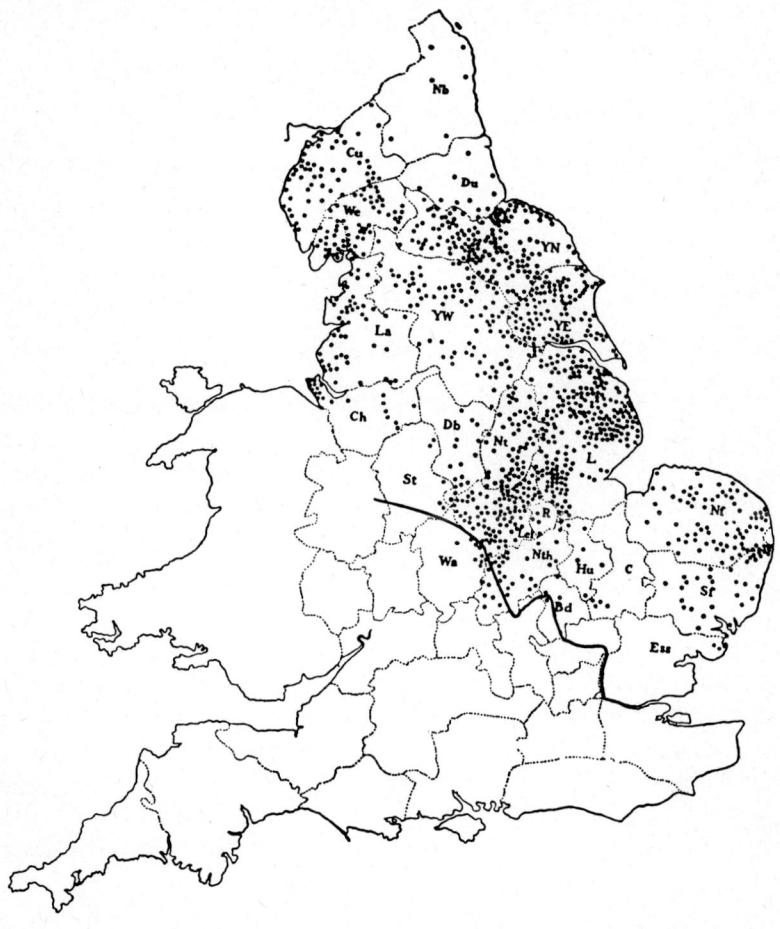

Scandinavian place-names in England, parish names of Scandinavian origin. (A. H. Smith, English Place-name Elements; English Place-name Society, vols. XXV-VI, 1956, map.)

been in Norway". Out of approximately 4500 runic inscriptions preserved from the Viking period and the following centuries, the majority date from the crucial time between 800 and 1050.

How can *place-names* and *personal names* throw light on the Danish and Norse settlements in overseas areas, such as the British Isles? Any traveller to northeastern England or to Ork-

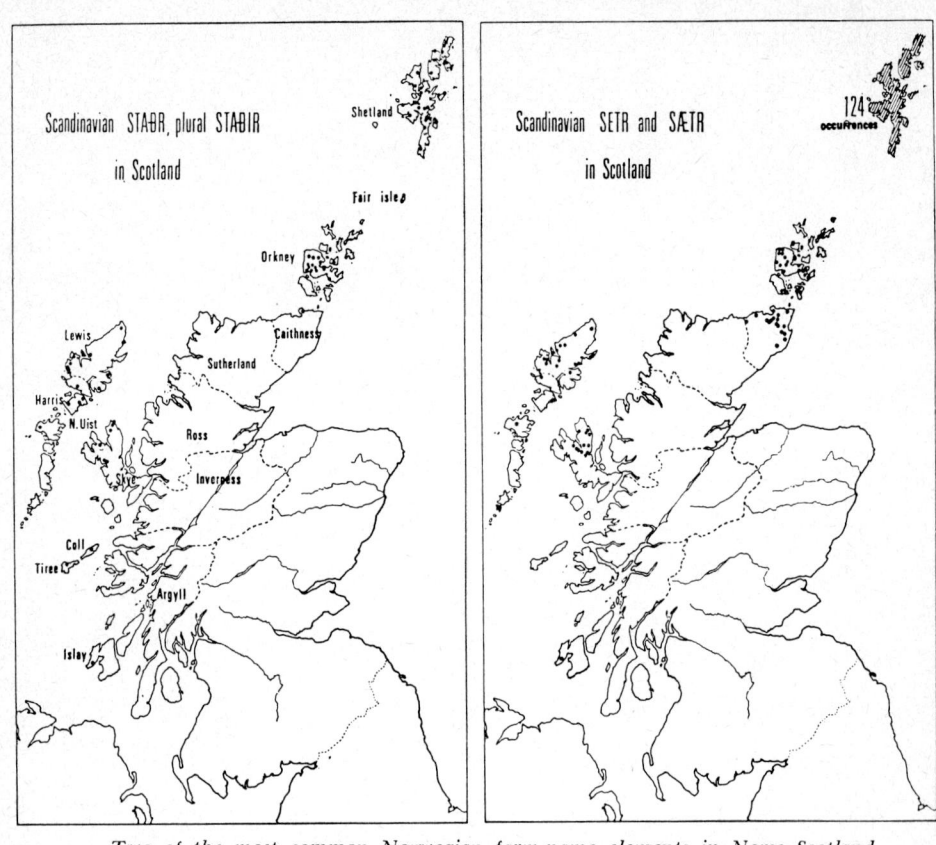

Two of the most common Norwegian farm-name elements in Norse Scotland -staðir and -setr. (W. F. H. Nicolaisen, Norse settlement in the Northern and Western Isles, The Scottish Historical Review, vol. 48 (1969), maps 1 and 2.)

ney will be struck by the frequent occurrence of compound place-names ending in -by (-bae, -bea), -thorp, -setter, -land, -bister, and -ston (-sta). The same place-name elements are to be found in Scandinavia and are in most cases incompatible with the earlier toponymical custom in the British Isles. Thus the study of such place-names, as the English historian P. H. Sawyer writes, "can reveal something of the origin of the settlers, and it can indicate much more precisely than the [Anglo-Saxon] Chronicle where those settlements were." The limitation of the place-name material, he adds, is that it "cannot define the exact

A Viking burial site excavated at Skedsmo, Ullensaker, southeastern Norway. (Universitetets Oldsaksamling, Oslo.)

extent of the first settlements any more than it can reveal the number of settlers — —." Frequently the origin of the settlers can be determined with greater reliability when the place-name has a personal-name element prefixed to it, as for example Grimsby, Germiston and Colster. These English and Orkney farm-names contain Norse (and Danish) personal names: Grim, Geirmund and Koll.

By far the richest storehouse of knowledge about the Viking Scandinavians and their culture is *the archaeological remains,* to be found scattered over a vast area, from Russia to Greenland and even Newfoundland, from the Mediterranean to the coast of northern Scandinavia. The graves and the dwelling-sites at a superficial glance seem to reveal very much the same picture of the material culture of our ancestors. However, when we consider the different functions of the grave and the dwelling-place, it is evident that they give the historians the opportunity to study both the social conditions of the living and the ideas connected with death. The gravefinds of Norway and in the Norse settlements along the coasts and on the islands of the North Atlantic reveal convincingy how the Vikings before their conversion to Christianity were expected to spend their life in the next world: weapons, farm equipment, kitchen utensils, clothes (textile fragments), ornaments, all testify to a rather practical conception of problems facing men in the life hereafter.

But the graves can also give evidence of the faith of the interred and throw light on the gradual conversion of the Vikings to Christianity. The cessation of grave goods in the graves is interpreted as a result of victorious Christianity, and the occasional finds of amulets, as for example the hammer of Thor or the Christian cross, may indicate the religious attitude of the owner.

Viking grave-finds in Scandinavia may quite frequently contain grave-goods of foreign origin. The numerous graves of the ninth, tenth, and eleventh century excavated in Norway, have produced a variety of objects of Anglo-Saxon, Irish, Frankish and Arabian origin. How should such finds be interpreted? It may often be difficult to decide whether objects of ornamental metalwork, bronze bowls, glass goblets, penannular brooches, or balance scales have come to Norway as a result of peaceful trade or as booty in the possession of Viking raiders. The concentration of grave finds with such western European objects in certain parts of Norway (e.g. Rogaland and Vestfold) at least indicates a brisk cultural contact with western Europe. The finds can, however, reveal little about the causes of this contact.

In this respect dwelling sites may give important additional information. They may tell us more directly where and how the Viking Scandinavians lived abroad. Are their settlement sites chiefly to be found within, or in the vicinity of present-day towns? Are they urban in character, or mainly to be located in rural areas? It is a matter of course that such questions can hardly be submitted to a rewarding statistical analysis, but they can give us information, indicating a general tendency. In Ireland and Russia the dwelling sites of the Vikings seem to be located near or within present-day towns, whereas excavations in Scotland, Orkney, the Faeroes and Iceland have almost

A soapstone mould from Himmerland, northern Jutland, Denmark. Pagan and Christian symbols side by side: the hammer of Thor and the Cross. (National-museet, Copenhagen.)

exclusively brought to light sites of a rural character. In Scandinavia the finds of dwellings from the Viking period are of such a character as to make generalizations about settlement difficult. The more interesting groups of finds here are Viking market places and church sites, the latter establishing beyond doubt the victorious progress of Christianity in the 11th century.

Modern historians of the Vikings have been especially attracted by the contemporary abundance of silver in Scandinavia and in the Viking settlements overseas. Their interest is especially concentrated upon *coins,* found in hoards or in single finds. The total number of coins from the Viking period found in Scandinavia can now be put at more than 230,000. They are almost exclusively of foreign provenance: Arabic (or Kufic), Anglo-Saxon, Frankish, German and Byzantine coins dominate the finds until about 1050.

Coins as source material for the study of the Vikings have come into the foreground in the post-war years, and the historians are greatly indebted to the pioneer research of the late professor Sture Bolin of the University of Lund. His great thesis of the dominant part of the Vikings in European affairs, especially as promoters of trade between the Orient and western Europe, rests essentially on thorough numismatical studies.

The flow of coins from other countries to Scandinavia bet-

The 9th-century Soma grave find from Jæren, southwestern Norway, containing Irish-style mountings. (Universitetets Oldsaksamling, Oslo.)

ween 800 and 1050 follows an interesting pattern. Before 950 Kufic coins have a dominant position in most coin hoards to be found in Scandinavia. After the middle of the 10th century the coin stream changes direction, and now most of the coins are from German and Anglo-Saxon mints. What is the explanation of this conspicuous change? How should we interpret the coin finds in terms of trade and booty?

We have so far not included *the sagas* and *the old laws* of the Northmen in our review of sources. Severe historical criticism has reduced the sagas to legends, in part presented as great literature. And the laws, although considered valuable as reflecting the social and legal conditions of the Scandinavians, do not

Coins illustrating the cultural and economic contacts of the Vikings: 1. A Kufic dirhem issued by a Samanid prince at Tashkent A.D. 897/98 and found at Holtan, Orkdal in Sør-Trøndelag. — 2. A Bryzantine solidus issued by Constantine VII and Romanus II A.D. 945/59 in Byzantium and found at Nedre Strømshaug, Råde in Østfold. — 3. An Anglo-Saxon penny isued by King Eadgar in the second half of the 10th century and found at Årstad, Egersund in Rogaland. — 4. A Frankish denier of the XPISTIANA RELIGIO-type issued by Louis the Pious (814—40) and found at Kaupang, Tjølling in Vestfold. (Universitetets Myntkabinett, Oslo.)

offer an easy approach for the students of the Viking period, since very few of their provisions can with certainty be dated back to this time. Neither sagas nor laws are strictly contemporary, whereas in this book we are concerned first and foremost with the evidence of the time. But when this has been said, it must be admitted that the sagas in places may give a general impression of the spirit of the Viking age, and it is also fair to say that the old laws may throw light on the social attitude of Viking man.

II. NORSEMEN ABROAD AND NORSEMEN AT HOME, THE PICTURE GIVEN BY ARCHAEOLOGY

At Knoc-y-Doonee near the north coast of the Isle of Man, in a region where Norse place-names are not uncommon, a burial-mound was opened in 1928. It turned out to contain a Norse boat-grave which could be dated back to the early 10th century. To judge from about 300 iron rivets found on the site, the boat must have been some 30 feet long, 8 feet wide, and 3 feet high. The man who had been put to rest in the boat, had been well furnished for his passage to the realm of death. The weapons (a sword, a spear-head and an axe), a bronze pin and a buckle, and fragments of a leather strap with bronze mountings were found in the middle of the boat. Some 5 or 6 feet farther away were found an iron bowl with a knife alongside it, together with some equipment indicative of the man's different pursuits: a hammer, a smith's tongs, another knife, and a sinker for a fishing line. In the stem were some greatly decayed fragments of horsebones, some iron buckles, links, and fragments of a harness. This find may be regarded as a typical Viking grave of the Norse settlements in the West. It was probably a well-to-do farmer over whom the mound was raised.

The Norsemen who settled in the Isle of Man had found their way through the archipelago of northwestern Scotland. On April 26th 1915 an inspector of schools in the island of Lewis of the Outer Hebrides was visiting the school at Valtos, a windswept little place on the west coast facing the Atlantic. The headmaster of the school drew his attention to "certain articles of brass and bronze" which some of the school children had recently unearthed from a small sand mound. About 150 feet from the school in a patch of sandy soil a boy had noticed a bone sticking out of the ground, and together with his friends he started digging and made one of the most exquisite Viking finds in Scotland. The objects belonged to a woman's grave and consisted of a pair of tortoise brooches of an early Norwegian

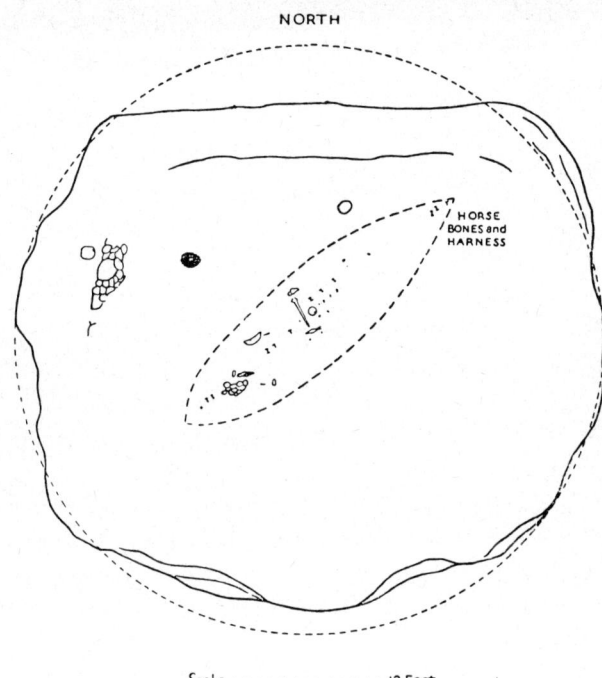

*The boat-burial at Knoc-y-Doonee, Isle of Man. Plan of mound.
(After The Antiquaries' Journal X (1930), p. 127.)*

type, a circular bronze brooch, ornamented in Celtic style, and with a setting for amber or a stone in the middle, a bronze belt-buckle, a penannular brooch, a bronze chain, an oblong bead of reddish-brown amber, and some remains of iron objects. The find clearly evinces the mingling of Norse and Celtic influences and has been dated to the second half of the 9th century.

From the Butt of Lewis past Cape Wrath to Rora Head in Hoy, one of the Orkney islands, is a distance of slightly less than 110 miles of straight sailing in the open Atlantic. These islands to the north of Scotland are a real El Dorado for the archaeologist and for the student of Norse place-names, but the finds of Viking graves are not impressive. In the northwestern island of Westray close to the village of Pierowall (O. N. *Hǫfn*)

Tortoise brooch, fragment of shield boss, and penannular brooch from graves at Pierowall, Orkney. (The National Museum of Antiquities of Scotland, Edinburgh.)

a whole cemetery of heathen Viking graves was excavated in the middle of the 19th century. In addition to the traditional equipment found in the graves of both sexes, six out of some 20 grave finds in this area were undoubtedly boat-graves, as could be inferred from the presence of numerous boat rivets in the burial-ground. In the Pierowall area there must have been a relatively dense Norse settlement, but no dwelling sites have so far been uncovered. However, such sites have been excavated in recent years at Buckquoy and Brough of Birsay, Mainland, Orkney, and at Westness, Rousay.

In the Orkneyinga Saga it is told how Earl Ragnvald of Orkney, the founder of the St. Magnus Cathedral, on his way back from Norway in 1148 was shipwrecked in the southern part of the Shetland Mainland, and how during his involuntary stay there he helped an old *bonde* or farmer of Sumburgh Voe (*Dynrastarvágr*) to catch fish. The place is described as quite populous, and the author of the Orkneyinga Saga mentions "many poor folk" among the fishermen-farmers. Norwegian Vikings on their way home from raids in Scotland and along

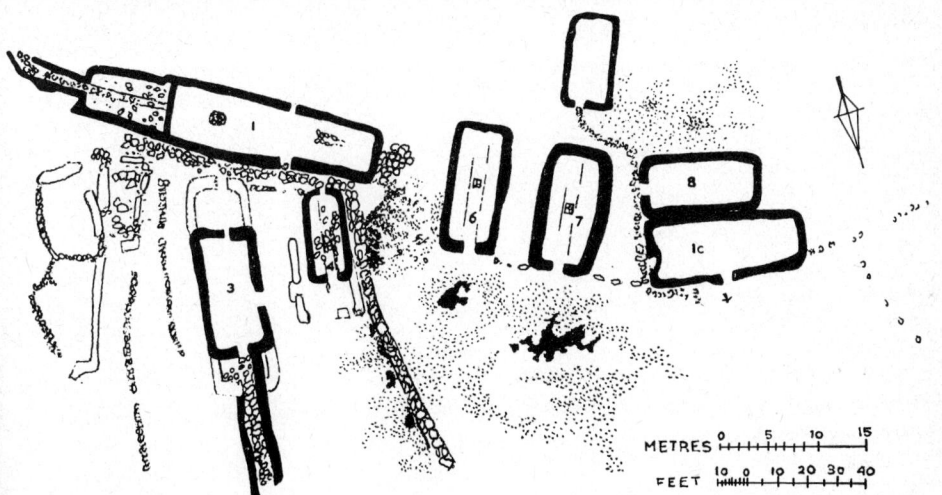

11th-century dwelling sites at Jarlshof, Shetland, with traces of older buildings from the early Viking period. (J.R.C. Hamilton, Excavations at Jarlshof, fig. 72 facing p. 155.)

the coasts of the Irish Sea are likely to have made their crossing from Pierowall to Sumburgh Voe. In this hamlet they would find their first safe haven in the Shetland archipelago.

Since 1897 the excavations of a big mound here on the shores of the West Voe have brought to light an extensive area of settlement belonging to different prehistoric and historic periods. Remains of an oval, stone-built hut of the Neolithic age have been uncovered. It was followed by a village of the Bronze age, a Broch settlement of the early Iron age, a Norse hamlet spanning the whole period from about 800 until the 12th or 13th century A.D., and finally by a late mediaeval farmstead and a laird's hall ("Jarlshof").

The stripping of the Norse farmsteads was undertaken in two periods between 1936 and 1952, and the excavations have so far produced eight houses, three or possibly four of which can be dated to the Viking age. The parent house from the beginning of the 9th century suggests a building of the traditional type, common in southwestern Norway. It has been a longhouse some 60 by 20 feet with two hearths. Originally it probably gave room both to the settlers and their animals. A little later in the same century, a byre, a smithy and possibly a bath house seem to have been built not far from the dwelling-house. Objects found on the sites of the Viking Age houses mostly indicate peaceful farming and fishing pursuits, although an occasional find highlights the central position of Sumburgh Voe (or Jarlshof) on the Viking route from Norway to the British Isles. An incised slate bore the representation of a ship with close resemblance to the pre-viking Kvalsund boat. Fragments of steatite bowls are quite numerous, and some fragments of cooking bowls have incised grooves below the rim. This type is quite common in southwestern Norway, and together with steatite loomweights they may represent importation from Norway, although steatite is not uncommon in Shetland. There are also some finds indicating a certain contact with other parts of the British Isles. Several bronze pins and an Irish harness-mount may bear witness to Viking visitors on their way home. But there is little likelihood of Sumburgh Voe having served as an important pirate base in the Viking centuries.

The distance between Shetland and the nearest islands of Norway south of the Sognefjord is about 220 miles. And it is almost certain that most Viking raiders returning home would prefer to go due east and that most of them would make their landfall somewhere in this area. Having gained the safety of the island-sheltered coast, they would easily find their bearings northwards or southwards in the coastal waters. But where do we find the homes to which these Norsemen returned with booty or from which they went out to trade? It would be easy to generalize: The Vikings lived in almost every *vik* or bay along the coast of Norway which had suitable landing possibilities and where there was some tillable soil. But such a generalization would not give a very clear picture of the central areas in the Norwegian homeland engaged in Viking activities. What can contemporary evidence tell us about every-day life in those areas which seem to have been politically most active in Norway during the Viking period?

At Hetland in the southwestern district of Jæren, near the city of Stavanger and in an area abounding in Viking and earlier

Dynrastarvágr (Jarlshof) as it might have appeared on a busy day in the heyday of Viking expansion. A reconstruction by the artist Alf Næsheim (artist's copyright).

prehistoric graves, a mound was uncovered about a hundred years ago. It turned out to be a richly equipped grave from the second half of the 9th century, and as such it is quite common in the Jæren district. What calls for our special attention in this find, however, is the beautifully ornamented harness mountings of gilt bronze and the tin-coated bronze mountings of drinking-horns. Together with these objects were also found an iron bridle bit, a pair of tortoise brooches, two silver arm-rings, six pearls of exquisite workmanship, a frying pan and a spit, a bronze cauldron, two knives, two iron clasps, a buckle and some rivets. The twelve harness and two drinking-horn mountings are all in Irish style and most definitely of Irish origin. The cauldron and the beads are also of foreign provenance. The woman in this grave had been sumptuously furnished with Irish ornamental pieces, probably brought home as booty. But she was not alone in benefiting from the raids in such a lavish way. The district of Jæren with some 30 'Irish' grave finds is the area which has the strongest concentration of finds containing ornamental metal work in Irish style (harness mountings and personal ornaments, largely torn from holy books and reliquaries) in the whole of Scandinavia. The only districts in Norway with comparable concentrations of Irish objects are Sogn og Fjordane (25 finds), Trøndelag (som 20 finds), and Vestfold (some 20 finds).

In the populous and flourishing Jæren district the decisive battle for the unification of Norway was fought c. 885 A.D. In the battle of Hafrsfjord King Harald Fairhair of Vestfold defeated local kings with Viking support from the British Isles. His ambition had brought him to Trøndelag and to western Norway from his own realm in the southeastern part of the country. This realm, Vestfold with its adjoining inner districts of Vest-Opplandene, is another splendid field for the archaeologist. Here is to be found the site of an important Norse trading centre, first mentioned in the writings of King Alfred of Wessex. Sometime about the year 880 a Norwegian trader and farmer *(farbonde)* came to King Alfred and went into his service. He gave the king a report of the geography of Scandinavia, which was reproduced by King Alfred in Anglo-Saxon in his translation of Orosius' History of the World. Ottar (Othere) related to the king that he lived in a district called Halgoland (Hålogaland). "He said that no one lived farther north than he did. Then there is a port (A.S., án port) in the southern part of the country which is called Sciringes heal. Thither he said that one might sail in less than a month if one camped by night and had favourable winds every day. — — — South of Sciringes heal a large sea [i.e. part of Skagerak and the Oslo fjord] runs up into the country. The sea is wider there than any man can see across. — — — And from Sciringes heal he said that he sailed for five days to that port which is called *æt Hæþum* [i.e. Hedeby]."

The port of Sciringes heal or Skiringsal was in 1850 identified by the historian Peter Andreas Munch as a tract of land belonging to the farm *Kaupang* on the shores of the Oslofjord less than two miles east of the present town of Larvik. In a letter to an Orkney friend he mentions that he has found the cemetery of the town, consisting of "almost an immense number of barrows,

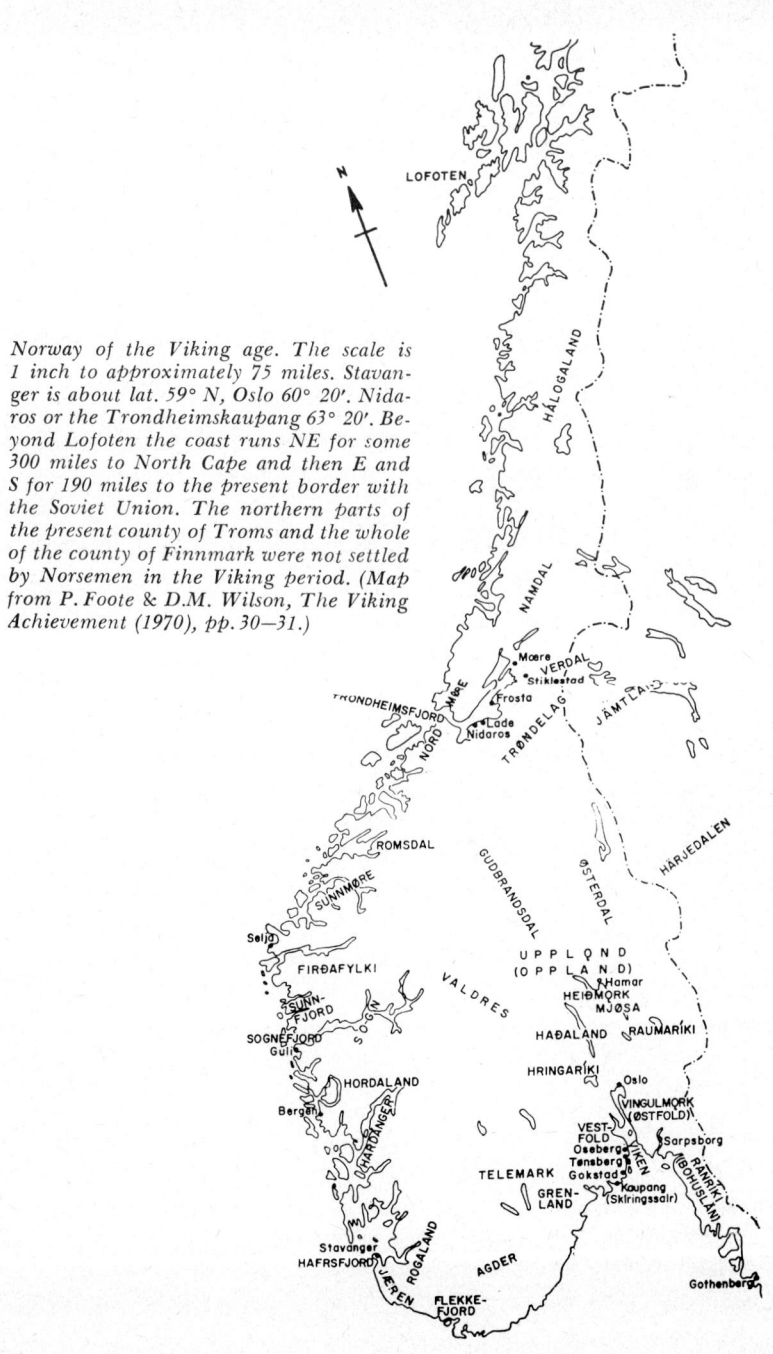

Norway of the Viking age. The scale is 1 inch to approximately 75 miles. Stavanger is about lat. 59° N, Oslo 60° 20'. Nidaros or the Trondheimskaupang 63° 20'. Beyond Lofoten the coast runs NE for some 300 miles to North Cape and then E and S for 190 miles to the present border with the Soviet Union. The northern parts of the present county of Troms and the whole of the county of Finnmark were not settled by Norsemen in the Viking period. (Map from P. Foote & D.M. Wilson, The Viking Achievement (1970), pp. 30—31.)

large and small, many of them containing iron swords, glass beads, and remnants of boats — — —". Since 1950 the Kaupang area has been subjected to systematic excavations under the leadership of Mrs. Charlotte Blindheim, Curator of the Museum of National Antiquities, Oslo. A greater part of the cemeteries and a fraction of the urban area (the black soil area) have been uncovered, revealing an interesting market place, probably of permanent character and a trade centre for the petty kingdom of the Yngling royal line, to which Harald Fairhair is supposed to have belonged. Even before the more comprehensive excavations of the 1950's the cemeteries had produced a series of interesting artefacts, such as Frankish swords of the Ulfberht make, a large number of steatite cooking pots and fragments of balance scales, the last group giving some indication of the preoccupation with trade. The material from the excavations of recent years, however, in the extensive and densely populated cemetery of Bikjhol-bergene and in a minor part of the settlement area has completely overshadowed all earlier finds. It is certainly sufficient to establish Skiringsal, or rather Kaupang, not only as a port, but as a main trading centre in Scandinavia. The remarkably great concentration of boat graves of the inhumation type at this locality, seen on the background of other extensive 9th century-cemeteries in the area, has given further support to the theory that Kaupang was a permanent settlement of urban character. There seems to have been a relatively strong element of traders who had contacts with European coastal emporia, an impression that is strongly corroborated by the finds in the black soil area. The most representative groups of foreign artefacts are the pottery sherds, pointing to Western Germany, the book and reliquary mountings of Anglo-Irish origin, numerous exquisitely-made imported beads, brooches from Eastern Scandinavia (the town of Birka?), and an important little collection of coins (c. 30 single finds from the black soil) with Kufic coins as the dominant group.

This coin material probably gives us the best illustration of Kaupang's widespread contacts. The c. 20 Kufic coins have most likely arrived here from the Orient by way of Sweden

(Uppland or Gotland), and the Hedeby coin is probably of Danish provenance. The two Frankish deniers of Louis the Pious (814–840) and the two Anglo-Saxon pennies of Coenwulf of Mercia (796–822) must be seen against the background of Viking activity in the British Isles and France. In this coin material we have an indication of the main direction of Viking trade and intercourse during the 9th century: the East-West route between the Baltic and the coastal waters of western Europe.

But Viking activity was not limited to the coastal districts of southern Norway. Trøndelag, the relatively fertile region around the Trondheim fjord, was also taking an active part in the general economic and political expansion of Norway. It has generally been considered by historians to have played a less important part in the Viking expeditions and settlements than western and southeastern Norway. This hypothesis, however, rests mainly on written sources, and primarily on the Icelandic *Landnámabók,* which gives an enumeration of the leading settlers from Norway, who took land on Iceland. If we turn to the material which has hitherto formed the basis of our survey, the archaeological finds of the Viking period in Trøndelag are no less conspicuous than those of other regions of Norway. We should notice particularly its leading position as regards finds of Anglo-Irish mountings. In this period a town was founded at the mouth of the Nid river (later known as Nidaros), and Steinkjer at the bottom of the Trondheims fjord became an important market-place. But it is probably in the coin material that we have the clearest evidence of the engagement of the Trøndelag region in the Viking expansion. At least one-third of the approximate total of 400 Kufic (Arabic) coins found in Norway, have been found in Trøndelag.

In 1913 a coin hoard was found at the farm of Holtan in the valley of Orkdal, Sør-Trøndelag. It consisted of 64 Kufic silver coins in a good state of preservation, most of them issued at Tashkent and Samarkand in Central Asia between 896 and 950. Probably one of the most interesting coins found at Holtan was a dirhem issued in 949 by the prince of the Bulgars on the upper Volga in Russia. The main route of the Swedish traders

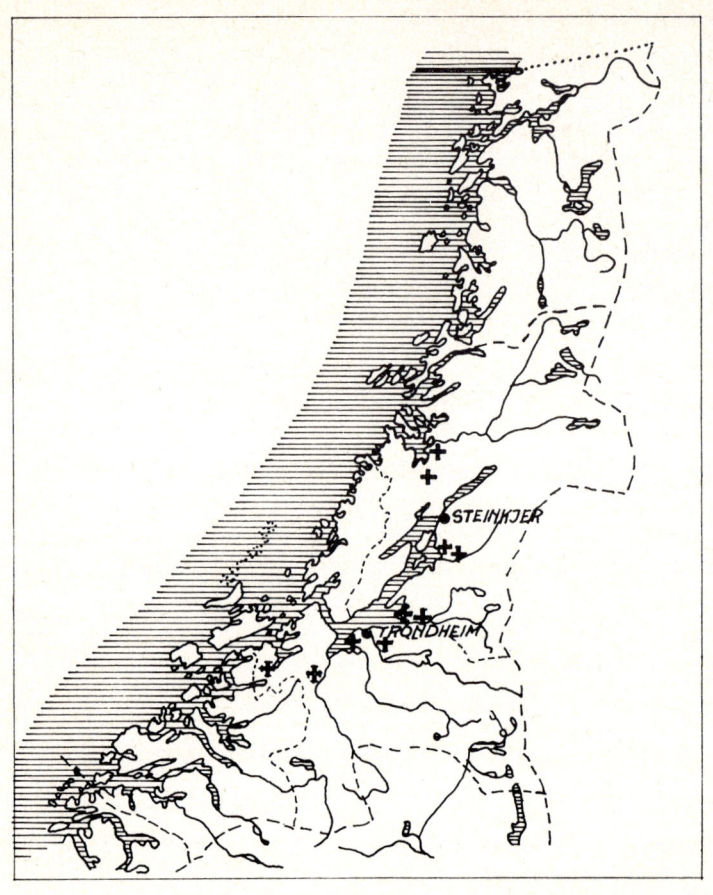

Kufic coin hoards and coin finds (marked with +) in Trøndelag. (Det Kgl. Norske Videnskabers Selskabs skrifter 1916, no. 9, plate IV.)

to the riches of the Orient in the 9th century was along the Volga river. The Holtan find is one of the biggest hoards of Kufic coins ever discovered in Norway. And it is not the only one in this region, as a total of about 115 coins has been found in 17 different finds (mostly hoards). There are only two other regions with a similar concentration of coins and finds: Vestfold with hinterland (80 coins, 6 finds) and Rogaland (31 coins, 7 finds). These very regions are exactly the ones in which we have found such clear evidence of contact with the Norwegian sphere of influence in western Europe. Thus in Norway, as in Sweden, the silver of the East and the products of the West have been found most strongly represented in the leading economic and political regions.

It is time to repeat Professor Sture Bolin's main question in a slightly modified version and one more adapted to the case of Norway: Did the silver of the Orient contribute essentially to the Viking expansion from Norway, or must we also take other factors into account, as for instance overpopulation? The answer to this question can hardly be given in a satisfactory way unless we make a closer observation of Viking activity at home as well as abroad. Only thus there may be some likelihood of finding out about the interplay between causes and effects.

So far we have followed the traces of Norse Vikings along the homeward route from the Irish Sea to some regions in Norway which seem to have taken a prominent part in the general movement between East and West and in the expeditions to the West: Rogaland (southwestern Norway), Vestfold (southeastern Norway) and Trøndelag. The various objects found in the graves, the hoards, and the dwelling-sites have given us a cross-section of material illustrating everyday life in most strata of Viking society abroad and at home. The Knoc-y-Doonee boat-grave in the Isle of Man gives the impression that an apparently successful Norseman of the early 10th century, one who belonged to the first or second generation of Irish Sea settlers, was not only occupied with raiding. He evidently had rather full days of peaceful work on his farm. — The woman who was interred at Valtos, Lewis, in the Outer Hebrides sometime during the second half of the 9th century may have belonged to the first settlers there, if we can accept the tortoise brooches as indicative of her ties with Norway. The brooches in Celtic style, however, show that Irish cultural influence was making itself felt at an early stage of settlement, or at least in the 9th century.

While the boat-grave of Knoc-y-Doonee and the woman's grave of Valtos can be clearly classified as Norse graves, they do not in themselves permit any conclusions as to the social conditions of the settlers at large in the islands where these people had found their last resting-place. The grave finds in the Isle of Man and the Hebrides are too few. In this respect the finds in Orkney and Shetland are of such a character as to give not only some indication of a stratified Norse society, but also of the main areas of Norse settlement. And above all they can point out certain population centres such as Pierowall (Hǫfn) and Jarlshof (Dynrastarvágr). Still it is not easy on the basis of the archaeological material from the graves and the settlement sites to say anything quite definite about the role played by the Orcadians and Shetlanders in the Viking expeditions against Ireland and England. There can be no doubt, however, about their contact with and dependence on the sea; and it is reasonable to conclude from the geographical situation of these islands that they must have had a function in the mass movement across the sea from Norway to western Europe as platforms for the Viking invasion of the British Isles.

The more comprehensive and systematic archaeological study of Viking Norway seems to point out some areas in this country as the leading regions in the expansion westward: southwestern Norway (especially Jæren), the Sognefjord and Møre areas, southeastern Norway (especially Vestfold) and Trøndelag with its outlying coastal districts. In these regions archaeology can give more than the cultural background of society in the 9th and 10th centuries, it can also suggest to the historian what were the main forms of Viking economic activity, and thus enable him to formulate such vital questions as: What were the prime motives of those people who took part in the expeditions from Norway to the West? Do the artefacts testify chiefly to the piracy of the Vikings, or is it more advisable to regard them as a result of an intercontinental or European trade between the East and the West? Again it may be easy or tempting to generalize: The Irish mountings in the rich graves of Jæren have probably been brought home as booty from the British Isles. The pottery sherds found at the site of the port of Kaupang in Vestfold have undoubtedly been the commodities of peaceful traders. The Kufic coins of the Holtan hoard have most likely been hidden away by some farmer-trader who feared the tyranny of a chieftain or a king.

We have arrived at the main limitations of archaeology: Although it furnishes us with a picture of Viking activities abroad and at home, archaeology can only tell us in general terms what activities predominated at particular times and in particular areas. At the same time it certainly gives the historian sufficient material to enable him to define *a Viking*.

III. THE VIKING AND HIS WAY OF LIFE

We should not hesitate to term a Viking a pirate or a warrior, but piracy and war were not his only occupations. He was also a farmer and a trader. And it is quite impossible to make a clear distinction between his warlike and peaceful doings. He might be a peaceful farmer in his home district during wintertime, whereas in summer he went out to raid foreign coasts. There is no agreement about the etymology of the old Norse word *vikingr*. We do not know whether it means a man from a bay (*vik*), fjord; a man of the camp; a man of the town; or a man who made a "tour away from home". But there is no doubt about the fact that in the Norse laws of the 13th century the word has the meaning of "pirate"—a man who violated the king's peace. Unfortunately we do not know whether this was the connotation or general meaning of the word in the 9th and 10th centuries. By modern historians it is used to denote both the men and the civilization of Scandinavia during the period from about 800 till about 1050. Women took part in the westward movement across the sea, and settlements would hardly have had any chance of surviving without them. The attacks and invasions launched on the British Isles would have been impossible without constant reinforcements from home. We find Norse Vikings in Norway as well as the British Isles, France, Iceland, Greenland, and further to the West, and in eastern Europe.
We find them as warriors, farmers, housewives, traders, artists, poets, chieftains, kings, priests, lawmen and sportsmen.

The Viking warrior.
   The battle of Fitjar in western Norway between King Hákon the Good and the sons of Eric Bloodaxe about 960 has been recorded both in skaldic poetry and in saga. Snorre Sturlason in *Heimskringla* has been able to base his description of the battle directly on a contemporary source, the skald Eyvind

The battle of Hafrsfjord as represented by the artist Erik Werenskiold. (Snorre Sturlason, (Heimskringla) Kongesagaer, ed. A. Holtsmark & D.A. Seip (1964), p. 61.)

Skaldaspiller's poem *Hákonarmál:* "When King Hákon had drawn up his men, it is told of him that he threw off *his armour* before the battle began. — — — King Hákon selected willingly such men for his guard or hird as were distinguished for their strength and bravery, — — —; and among these was Toralv Skolmsson the Strong, who went on one side of the king. He had *helmet* and *shield, spear* and *sword;* and his sword was called by the name of Footbreadth. — — — When both lines met there was a hard combat, and much bloodshed. The men threw their spears, and then drew their swords." Snorre then goes on to tell how the king killed a great Viking with his sword Quernbiter and how he was wounded in the pursuit of the enemy army: "Then flew an *arrow,* one of the kind called *flein* [arrow with hooks], into Hákon's arm, into the muscles below the shoulder." According to Snorre this wound proved fatal.

As a general description of a Viking battle this is as reliable as that of any other contemporary skald. It gives in simple words the tactics employed as well as a list of the equipment used by the warriors.

Helmet, of an archaic type found in a 10th-century chieftain's grave at Gjermundbu, Ringerike. (Universitetets Oldsaksamling, Oslo.)

We should bear in mind that the Norsemen fought all their battles on foot, though often arriving at the field of battle by ship or on horseback. In the battle of Fitjar both armies had come there by ship. Even such encounters as in modern terminology would nowadays be called naval engagements, were fought in the same way as a land battle. The ships rowed towards each other in two lines, and the ships of friend and foe were fastened one to the other by *tengsl,* ropes or similar devices. A combat on deck planks took place.

In the battle of Fitjar King Hákon, according to the skald, wore a golden *helmet.* The poet's statement should not be taken too literally, it is more likely that it was made of bronze or iron. Very few helmets from Viking age Scandinavia have come down to us. The only one found in Norway, the Gjermundbu helmet, is from a chieftain's grave at Ringerike, southern Norway, and can be dated to the 10th century. Although only fragmentary when excavated, it has been possible to reconstruct it. The helmet turned out to be of a somewhat archaic type, a "poor relation" of the famous pre-Viking Valsgärde-helmet found in Uppland, Sweden.—The winged or horned helmets

Helmets and mail-shirts of 1066 as represented by the artists of the Bayeux Tapestry.

have been created by imaginative, romantic 19th-century writers and are non-existent in the Viking age. It is likely that the plain conical helmet was fashionable among the upper warrior class (cf. the Bayeux Tapestry), but it was certainly no part of the ordinary man's equipment.

Mail-shirts have been found in a few Viking age graves in Norway (e.g. at Gjermundbu). They were probably rare in the early Viking period, and were undoubtedly reserved for men of distinction or for a king's *hirdmenn* (retainers).—The ordinary means of protection against the spears, swords, axes and arrows of the enemy was the round wooden *shield*. The shield boards were held together by an iron rim along the edge and by one or more iron bars at the back, constituting at the same time a grip for the hand, which again was protected by an iron boss on the front. The frequent finds of shield bosses in graves suggest that the shield must have been standard equipment for the warrior-farmer of the time.

According to a provision in the old Norwegian Laws every free man should attend a weapon *thing* with a spear, a broadaxe or sword, and a shield. They are termed folk weapons.—

Shield from the Gokstad ship. (Universitetets Oldsaksamling, Oslo.)

Apart from the shield *the spear* was probably the most common of these weapons. We may distinguish between two main types: the javelin with a thin and light blade and the thrusting spear or lance with a broad and heavy blade. Javelin blades, although varying in size and shape, were usually made of plain iron, whereas lance blades might be damascened or patternwelded, and their shaft sockets were not infrequently ornamented with inlaid silver. There are frequent mentions of the use of spears of both types in the sagas: The Viking king Olav Tryggvesson was able to throw javelins with both hands at the same time, and Olav Haraldsson, the saint king of Norway, received one of his fatal wounds from the chieftain Tore Hund's thrusting spear.—Spears then seem to have been used by everybody regardless of rank, the same is in all probability the case with the *battleaxe* or *broad-axe,* the heavy, longhandled, triangular-bladed weapon which needed two hands to wield it. According to Snorre Sturlason Thorstein the ship-smith inflicted the first serious wound on King Olav with his axe, and the third and final stroke may have come from the chieftain Kalv Arneson's broad-axe. The Norsemen seem to have regarded their

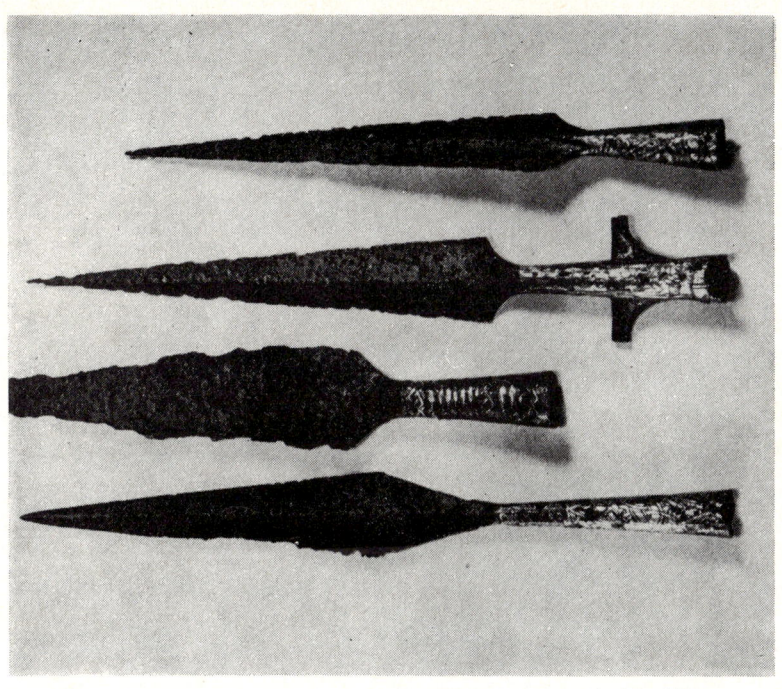

Spear-heads with silver-ornamented sockets (B. Almgren et al., The Viking (1966), p. 225.)

axes with a certain affection and respect, to judge from epithets like *Steinsnaut* (Stein's gift) and *Hel* (Death).—The weapon most likely to be found in the hand of a king or a chieftain during a fight, would be *the sword*. No other weapon of the period has been studied with greater care and perseverance than the sword; and the Norwegian archaeologist Jan Petersen in his classical work on "The Viking Swords of Norway" (1919) has not only established a reliable typology, but he has also graded the different groups chronologically, thus furnishing the student of Viking culture with an indispensable tool for dating finds and objects. Because of the relatively intricate and time-consuming process of production, the sword was probably the most expensive and the most treasured of the Viking's weapons. Although a great many of them were brought home from the Frankish empire (e.g. the name-ornamented Ulfberht swords),

41

Inlaid iron axe from Mammen, Jutland, Denmark (Nationalmuseet, Copenhagen.)

it is generally agreed among Norwegian archaeologists that the bulk of the Viking swords, especially the simpler ones, were produced in Norway. The Norse weapon-smiths were first-class craftsmen, and they knew how to harden the blade. It is possible that they also mastered the more complex technique of damascening and patternwelding, in which the sword-blade was built up partly by welding together several thin bars of iron and steel, partly by welding twisted steel bars on top of the main iron bar, so as to create a pattern along the blade. During the 10th century pattern-welded swords were replaced by swords of an improved damascening technique in which parallel laminations of pure iron and steel gave a tougher, more flexible and lighter product. In the sagas and in skaldic poetry the

Swords of the Vikings. (B. Almgren et al., The Viking (1966), p. 222.)

swords are not only described as precious gifts and heirlooms, but they are also credited with magic power. The striking resemblance between the pattern on a snake's back and the pattern-ornament on the sword struck contemporaries and inspired them with admiration and awe. The Viking looked upon his sword as his trusted friend and frequently gave it a name indicating its quality (as e.g. "Quernbiter", "Legbiter", "Footbreadth", etc.).—According to the saga descriptions of battles, *arrows* played an important part at the outset of each fight. The saga-writer seems constantly to refer to "showers of arrows through the air". In the above-mentioned provision from the old Gulathing Law (p. 39) about the folk weapons, the arrows are evidently considered as the collective responsibility of the farmers at the weapon *things:* "The freemen shall provide one bow and two dozen arrows for each thwart [of the coastal defence or *leidang* ship]."—We do not know much about *the Viking bow,* but it was certainly much smaller than the 12th century Welsh archer's longbow. The best bows were made from the yew-tree, and the bow god *(boga áss)* of Norse my-

*Arrows from a grave at Vågå, Gudbrandsdalen.
(Universitetets Oldsaksamling, Oslo.)*

thology, *Ullr,* had his home in *Ydalir,* the valleys of the yew tree. These weapons constitute the normal equipment of the Viking warrior, but it goes without saying that some of them were also used for more peaceful pursuits. The hunter probably pursued game with the same spear and the same bow as he brought along on the ship heading for foreign coasts.

The farmer.
Unlike Denmark and the greater part of southern Sweden, Norway's resources of tillable soil are small. The mountain valleys and rocky coasts of this country afford little opportunity

Archers at Hastings, 1066.

for extensive cultivation of cereals, and the soils of the lowland areas are not especially fertile. Nevertheless it is a remarkable fact that the best agricultural regions, Trøndelag, southwestern Norway (esp. Jæren) and southeastern Norway, were the leading ones both in the Viking expansion and in the political activity that brought about the unification of Norway.

We should also bear in mind that the Gulf-stream exerts a benign influence upon the climate of western Scandinavia (and upon islands of the North Atlantic such as Iceland and the Faeroes). And it is possible that the climate in the Viking period

45

was even more favourable than it is today. The medieval scholar Ari froði in his *Book of the Icelanders* (ca. 1125) speaks of the land between the coast and the mountains as forest-covered, whereas present-day Iceland is mostly treeless.

The main means of subsistence in parts of Norway, however, have been cattle-farming, fishing and hunting. The characteristic feature of the Norwegian countryside was (and still is) the single farm with enclosed infields and extensive outfields for grazing herds of cattle, sheep and goats. The *bønder* or farmers of a local district often had at their disposal a common land in the nearby forests or in the mountains for herding, logging, fishing and hunting. The communal life of the village was unknown in Norway. Activities like fishing, hunting and herding of animals in areas outside the farm fields were necessary additional elements in the economy of the Viking farmer. In the mountain bogs iron was found, and primitive iron furnaces were constructed for the smelting of this bog ore. The products of the sea like sealskins, walrus tusks, whalebone, feathers, the products of the forest such as squirrel skins, bearskins and other furs gave a surplus for barter and for trade.

Few houses from the Viking period have so far been found in Norway, but in the Norse islands of the Atlantic, Shetland, Orkney, the Faroes, Iceland and Greenland, the sites of Viking houses have been excavated, making it possible to follow the development of the Viking farm-house. We have already mentioned (p. 24 f.) the Jarlshof houses in Shetland, where the historian is in the fortunate position of having at his disposal dwelling sites not only from the Viking age, but also from later periods. It is fairly certain that the building tradition prevalent in western Norway was brought over by the settlers to the Atlantic islands, and the houses were constructed with thick walls of earth and stones. The roof was covered with sods and rested chiefly on two rows of poles, which also enabled the residents to make partitions and panellings. At the beginning of the Viking period the long-house was a common feature of the Viking settlement. It was a relatively big dwelling with curved sidewalls some 40 to 60 feet long and some 15 to 20 feet wide. In the early Viking period it gave shelter for people and cattle under the same roof.

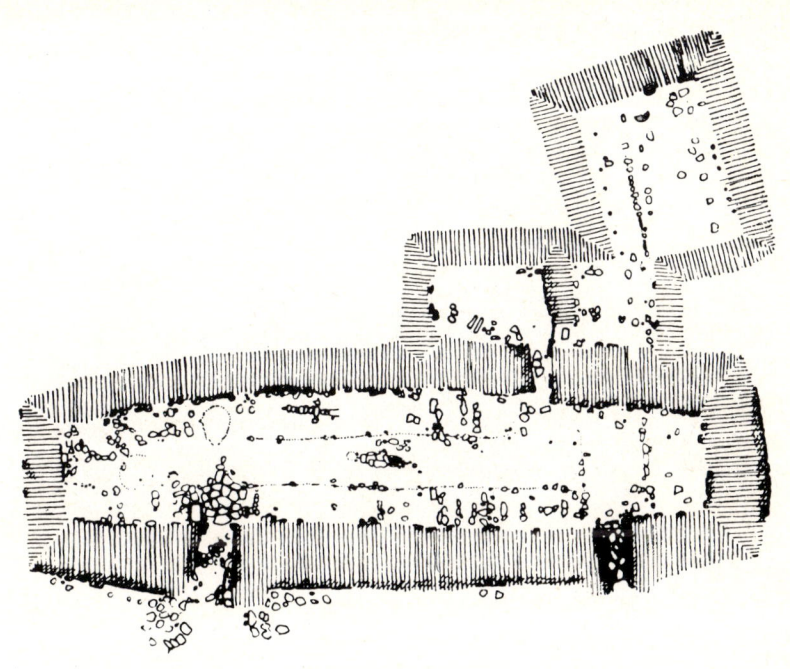

The Skalla-kot longhouse, Iceland, Aa. Roussel et al., Forntida gårdar i Island (1943), p. 58.

As time proceeded there was a development towards a more complex house pattern. The single long-house received additional rooms which were built on to it. And very soon separate houses were built for different purposes: a byre, a smithy, a bath house, etc. In Iceland at the farm-site of Skalla-kot we can follow the development from the single long-house to a dwelling of different rooms. The original longhouse has been partitioned into an entrance hall, a central main room and a kitchen area. The main room has raised earthen side-floors divided up by rows of stones. In the middle there is a long central hearth. The kitchen area or room has a cooking-pit and a separate doorway leading into it. Through a third doorway the farmer and members of his household had access to three more rooms. Thus the dwelling house gradually acquired separate rooms for various needs, as for example sleeping room, kitchen, storeroom, etc.

The burial chamber found in he Gokstad ship. Notice the cross-timbering at bottom. (Universitetets Oldsaksamling, Oslo.)

In the forest districts of southeastern Norway another building technique was introduced during the Viking period, namely cross-timbering. No Viking houses of this type have been preserved, although we may get an idea of how such a building was constructed from the burial chamber of the Gokstad ship. Stave-constructions also seem to have been well known before the erection of stave churches.

On the basis of different saga references it is possible to piece together the day's activities in a well-to-do farmer's house. The earliest time for rising in the morning seems to have been between four and five o'clock, the hour which was termed *rismál* in Old Norse. But there were undoubtedly many exceptions to the general rule, depending both on the season of the year and the nature of the work to be carried out. There seem to have been two principal meals. The first was called *dagverðr* or *dǫgurðr* and used to be taken some time before noon. After this meal it was usual to have a short rest. The other meal, *náttverðr* or night meal, was taken towards bedtime. Besides

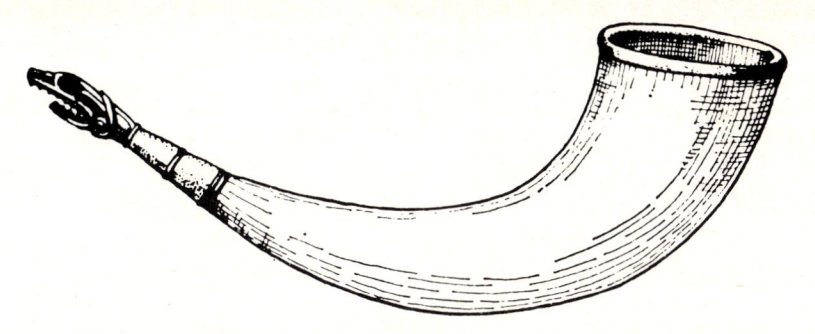

A drinking-horn. Reconstruction. (J. Simpson, Everyday Life in the Viking Age (1966), p. 73.)

these two meals there were most likely refreshments of some sort at other times during the day, but the sagas make no mention of such minor meals. The main meals were taken by the fireplace in the *skáli,* the dwelling house. The master of the house would take his "high seat", while the other members of the household seated themselves on long benches, the places close to the "high seat" being considered the most honourable. Narrow tables were put in front of the benches, and between them and the longfires (the hearth). The meal could then begin.

In the Viking household cauldrons, plates and knives were stock utensils, whereas forks were unknown. To a great extent fingers were relied on. The staple diet was probably some sort of porridge, mostly made of barley-meal, served in troughs; it was eaten with spoons of wood, horn or bone. Some sort of soft bread was also common. Milk and ale were often served in wooden cans or bowls, out of which they were drunk. Flesh and fish were eaten fresh or dried. Milk in the form of *skyr,* i.e. milk curdled and separated from the whey, was consumed at most meals. Ale was of course a favourite drink of the Vikings; at more festive occasions herb-flavoured mead was used, which according to saga tradition was quite potent. Drinking-horns or bowls were often used for such a noble beverage, the horns in particular being frequently ornamented with silver or bronze mountings. Ale or mead was especially drunk in quantity at the evening meal at which it was a common practice to continue drinking after the tables had been removed. The descriptions of drinking-bouts in the sagas more often than not seem to be introduced as preludes to murder.

How did the members of a farmer's household spend their time out of doors? Here we may let the incomplete Eddic poem *Rigspula* speak for itself. Although there is no general agreement about the date of its composition, it must reflect conditions of life in the Viking period, the more so as it seems to betray Irish influence. The poem tells how a god Ríg visited three different farms on earth, in each of which he stayed for a while, leaving behind progeny: a son by name of *Thrall* in the first house; in the second *Karl* (i.e. Carl) and in the third *Jarl* (i.e. Earl). As the names indicate, these three boys belonged to different social strata, and the poet has attributed to them activities characteristic of their rank. We are here primarily concerned with Karl the farmer and Thrall the slave. In a prosperous Viking farm it would be fairly common to find a mixed household of free men and serfs. According to *Rigspula**) Karl, the son born to the farmer's wife,

"— — — began to grow, and to gain in strength.
Oxen he ruled, and plows made ready,
Houses he built, and barns he fashioned,
And the plow he managed".

The poem also tells about the activities of Karl's step-father Afi and his wife Amma, who sat in their hall and "worked at their tasks":

"The man hewed wood for the weaver's beam;
His beard was trimmed, o'er his brow a curl,
His clothes fitted close; in the corner a chest.

— — — —

The woman sat and the distaff wielded,
At the weaving with arms outstretched she worked;
On her head was a band, on her breast a smock;
On her shoulders a kerchief with clasps there was."

*) Quotations from H. A. Bellows' edition of *The Poetic Edda*. N.Y. 1923.

Man's and woman's dresses, as represented on gold plaquettes ('gullgubber') found at Mære church, Trøndelag (Det Kgl. Norske Videnskabers Selskab, Museet, Trondheim.)

It is most likely that Karl and his parents worked their ample farm with the assistance of some thralls. How did this group of men without legal status live in Viking society? Ríg came to the cot of Ai and Edda, the two 'hoary' ones, who sat by the hearth in their 'olden' dress. Edda's son by Ríg, Thrall,

"— — — began to grow, and to gain in strength,
Soon of his might good use he made;
With bast he bound, and burdens carried,
Home bore faggots the whole day long."

He married *Thír* and by her had twelve sons, who were hard workers:

"Ground they dunged, and swine they guarded,
Goats they tended, and turf they dug."

The farmer's year was filled with the most varied activities. In spring after the snow had melted away, the cattle were taken out for the first time from the dark byre to graze on the young grass. Shortly afterwards ploughing of the fields and sowing of

51

cereal crops (oats, barley and more rarely wheat) started. The plough with the ploughshare, coulter, and some sort of mouldboard and the more primitive *ard* or scratch-plough were drawn more often by oxen than by horses.—But there were many other things to be done in spring at the farm: fencing, wood-cutting, peat-digging, dunging the fields with manure. In early summer the lambs were weaned, the sheep sheared and sent on to the pastures. In the Norwegian mountain valleys almost every farm had its shieling, some sort of a primitive farm establishment in the mountains where a good many of the household lived and worked during the summer months from about midsummer until about the autumnal equinox (23rd September). Cows, sheep, and goats were left to roam relatively freely in the hills around the shieling, but the cows in particular were looked after by herdsmen. From the milk of sheep, goats, and cows were made such dairy produce as butter, soft cheese, and *skyr* (see above p. 49). While he was in the mountains, the farmer took the opportunity to fish in the nearby lakes and rivers and to hunt in the more distant parts of the region; and in the Viking age game and fish seem to have been plentiful.

In the second half of July haymaking and the collection of twigs and bark began, and all this fodder was stored in barns; a good stock was necessary to save the animals during the winter months when most of them had to stay in the byres. August-September was harvesting time; and sheep, goats, and cattle were afterwards taken down from the mountains. The winter months from mid-October until mid-April were the period mostly for indoor activities, although some lumbering, fishing and hunting certainly took place during winter. This was a time of great activity for the housewife. Besides the ordinary housework she was also busy weaving, making clothes for the family and other members of the household, and taking part in the slaughtering of animals and the curing of flesh.

The activities of the Viking farmers seem to have been very much the same in Scandinavia as in the Viking colonies abroad, with some variations according to whether they lived along the coast or inland. But there were always more hazardous opportunities for the farmers to supplement their property from other sources. A Norse farmer of this period, especially if he had access to the sea, frequently spent his summers trading and raiding in foreign countries. It must have been a natural pattern of life in the coastal areas of Norway, the Northern Isles of Britain and the islands of the North Atlantic. This typical Viking tradition died hard, especially among the chieftain class. According to the Anglo-Saxon Chronicle a host of Norsemen came to southern England in 1046. They were led by two chieftains, Lodin and Erling, and attacked Sandwich with twenty-five ships. They "seized there indescribable booty, both in captives and in gold and silver". They also harried in Essex and then sailed east to Flanders and "sold there the spoil they had taken". Some twenty years later, according to the Orkneyinga Saga, a chieftain of Orkney, Svein Ásleivsson, tried to live up to the traditions of the past: "It was Svein's custom at that time to spend the winter at home in Gairsay, and he always kept eighty men there at his own expense. He had a drinking hall — — [there]. Svein always had a busy time in spring, and had a great deal of seed sown, and did a great deal of the work himself. But when this work was ended, he would go a-viking each spring, and would harry round the coasts of the Hebrides and Ireland, and he would come home at mid-summer. This he called "spring viking". Then he would stay at home until the grain was cut and the corn taken in. Then he would go a-viking, and not come back until a month after the beginning of winter [i.e. in November]. And that he called 'autumn viking'." Nothing is mentioned about his being concerned with trade, but we may note that Svein Asleivsson's last battle was fought in the streets of Dublin (c. 1170) in a vain attempt to recapture this rich Irish-Norse city of merchants.

The trader.
　The wealth of the Vikings was certainly to a great extent acquired by raiding and conquest. Only at rare intervals do the sources (foreign and Norse) give us glimpses of the active life of Viking traders, indicating another important source of this wealth. This activity, of course, went hand in hand with war. We have already mentioned the Norwegian trader Ottar

(*Othere*, see above p. 28), who in the 870's or 880's visited the port of Skiringsal in southern Norway, Hedeby in southern Jutland and King Alfred's court in Wessex. The king's rendering of Ottar's report is the classical description of a successful Norse trader, who almost always combined trade (and quite often piracy) with farming and other peaceful pursuits such as fishing and hunting. He certainly belonged to the chieftain class. "He was among the chief men of that land, although he had no more than 20 oxen and 20 sheep and 20 swine, and what little he ploughed, he ploughed with horses. But their riches mainly consist in the tribute which the Lapps pay them; this tribute is of animals' skins, birds' feathers, walrus ivory and ship-ropes that are made from hides of walrus or seals". Ottar was a farmer/trader like most of his countrymen. The articles he enumerated include both luxury goods and commodities in everyday use. Together with soapstone articles, dried fish, and possibly iron products they would cover the main items of Norwegian export during the Viking age.—Ottar not only furnishes the Viking historian with a very important list of commodities, but he also gives a clear description of one of the main arteries of Norwegian home and foreign trade, leading from the White Sea/Finnmark regions along the Norwegian coast to the Vik area of the south, and from such markets as Kaupang/Skiringsal farther on to Denmark, Sweden and northern Germany. Foreign merchants (e.g. Frisians) gave it the name of Norðweg—the northern way. But there was also a western way, and we have already "sailed" along most of this way from the Isle of Man past the north coast of Scotland, putting in at safe ports in Orkney and Shetland before crossing to the western coast of Norway.

How did a Viking merchant carry on his trade with foreign lands and markets? In Ottar's case he was evidently himself in charge of ship as well as cargo. But a more common practice among farmers who wanted to trade abroad, was to form a partnership, a *félag*. Two or more men pooled their goods and shipped them in their own ship to foreign markets to exchange for products needed at home. Even a king might join such a partnership as *félagi* (partner). *Heimskringla* (Saga of Olav the

Saint, ch. 66) tells the story of a man from Agder, called Gudleik Gerdske: "He was a great merchant, who went far and wide by sea, was very rich, and drove a trade with various countries. He often went east to Gardarike [Russia], and therefore was called Gudleik Gerdske [the Russian]. This spring [probably about 1018] Gudleik fitted out his ship, and intended to go east in summer to Gardarike. King Olav sent a message to him that he wanted to speak to him; and when Gudleik came to the king he told him he would go in partnership with him, and told him to purchase some costly articles which were difficult to be had in this country. Gudleik said that it should be according to the king's desire". We also hear what sort of goods the king wanted from Russia. "Gudleik went in summer eastwards to Novgorod, where he bought fine and costly clothes, which he intended for the king as a state dress; and also precious furs, and remarkably splendid table utensils." Gudleik was certainly not the only Norwegian trading with eastern Europe at this time. The way to the east, to the Baltic and to Russia, seems to have been a popular route in the late 10th and the first half of the 11th century. Not only traders went to Gardarike (Russia), it also became a favourite resort for princes of the Norwegian royal family. It is not unlikely that these political contacts were a result of traditional commercial connections not only between Sweden and Russia, but also between Norway and Russia. It goes without saying, however, that commercial activity between western Europe and Norway was much stronger throughout the entire Viking period. The Norwegian farmer/trader went first and foremost to the British Isles.

The deeper implications of what trade meant to Norway (and Scandinavia) may probably be gathered from looking at the old Norwegian laws. We find separate sections for Market Law (the *bjarkeyjar réttr*) and Merchant Law (the *farmanna lǫg*). And when we read the rather detailed and specific clauses or paragraphs of these laws, bearing in mind at the same time the obvious importance of coins and silver bullion, the evidence for a wide and brisk commercial activity carried on by a great many Norwegians, is indisputable. At times we even find saga statements to the effect that trade was considered more rewarding than warlike activities. There is a dialogue in Egil Skallagrimsson's saga between the chieftain Brynjolv of Aurland and his son Björn: "— — when spring came, then Brynjolv and Björn were talking one day of their affairs. Brynjolv asked what Björn meant to do. Björn said that it was most likely that he would go away out of the land. "Most to my mind is it", said he, "that you should give me a long-ship and crew therewith, and I go a-viking." "No hope is there of this", said Brynjolv, "that I shall put in your hands a warship and strong force, for I know not but you will go about just what is against my wish; — — —. A merchant-ship I will give you, and wares withal: go you then southwards to Dublin. That voyage is now most highly spoken of."

At the king's court.
In this chapter we are not concerned with every Viking chieftain who adopted the royal title, but with the territorial kings of Norway in the Viking period, either as rulers of petty kingdoms before the unification of Norway (about 900) or as kings of Norway in the 10th and 11th centuries.

Konungr, the Norse word for king, simply means a 'man of noted or noble origin'. A kingdom was looked upon as the private property of the royal family, being termed the king's *oðal*. Within the royal family any man in the direct male line, legitimate or illegitimate, was eligible. But a pretender only became a legitimate king after he had received the homage of the free men at the local assemblies or *things*. This solemn act was termed *konungstekja* — the 'taking' of the king.

However, in the Viking period the authority and power of the king rested not only on the assent and support of the people, but also on his own military and economic resources. These resources were chiefly concentrated on royal farms within the realm. The king travelled constantly from farm to farm, as he was dependent on the products of the royal domain and on the food-rents contributed by the farmers of each district. In some instances we find the royal farms situated close to markets or town-like centres such as Kaupang in Vestfold and Kaupang (later Nidaros) in Trøndelag. It is evident that the king was able to benefit in some way from the trade going on at these places. And as long as the king took a more or less direct part in the Viking expeditions to the west, wealth derived from plunder seems also to have been an essential contribution to the royal resources.

The daily routine in the king's dwelling house or hall cannot have been very much different from that of a well-to-do farmer's home. But, of course, a greater number of individuals, and among them several persons of rank (such as local chieftains) were always to be found at the royal court, which accordingly involved a more extensive housekeeping. Even before the unification of Norway the petty kings would have a fair number of men round them—their retinue, in Old Norse termed *hirð* (borrowed from Anglo-Saxon *hired,* meaning 'family', 'household'). The *hirð* consisted, according to the saga tradition, in addition to the royal family, of different groups of men: the *hirðmenn,* the *gestir,* the *húskarls,* and the *þrælls.* Outside these groups, but often even included in them, one would find skalds and artists.— The *hirðmenn* were the professional warriors in the king's retinue and formed his bodyguard. From this highest-ranking group were taken the top royal officers such as the *stallari,* the marshal, and the *merkismaðr,* the standard-bearer. Besides their military duties the leading *hirðmenn* acted as the king's counsellors, and the marshal (the *stallari*) as the king's spokesman and as the representative of the *hirðmenn* before the king.—The *gestir* or 'guests' received half the pay of the *hirðmenn* and acted as a kind of constabulary, executing his justice and collecting his dues.—The *húskarls* or house-carls might be a common term for all men attached to the royal court, but it was also used to denote the king's servants. The *þrælls* or thralls were responsible for the heavy labour. In the Saga of Olav the Saint it is mentioned that in the first half of the 11th century the king's *hirð* or household consisted of sixty *hirðmenn,* thirty *gestir,* and thirty *húskarls.*

In the royal hall the king used to sit on his 'high seat'—on the higher long bench. Next to him sat his councillors and the more distinguished *hirðmenn.* (In the Christian period his *hirð*-bishop and his *hirð*-priests used to sit at his right-hand side.) The *stallari* or marshal was often found on the lower long bench opposite the king together with more *hirðmenn* and the *gestir*.

At the royal farm the food seems to have been prepared in a separate kitchen-building, termed *steikarahús,* where the cooks, mostly thralls or serfs, carried out their duties under the supervision of a head cook. The pouring out of the drinks was undertaken by servants named *skenkjarar* (pourers), who filled the drinking-horns with beer or mead from a large vessel and carried them round to the members of the *hirð* and to guests. The king would drink to such people in the hall as he wanted to honour. Quite often a man would drink with his neighbour and vie with him in seeing which could drink the most. The meals usually ended at a sign from the king. In the sagas this sign is at times considered a device whereby a stingy king could reduce food consumption at court. It is told of King Harald Hardradi that he would knock on the table with his knife, as soon as he had eaten as much as he wanted. The servants then immediately set about clearing the tables, so that many had to go away hungry. At drinking bouts, however, he seems to have been more liberal, for then nobody was allowed to shirk his drink.

The royal court was certainly the centre of cultural activities both in the period of the petty kingdoms and after the unification of the country. In the king's presence the skalds recited their poems, the artisans carried out their crafts, and the priests, in pagan and Christian times, officiated at religious gatherings. Any self-respecting Norse king would have one or more skalds attached to his court or his *hirð*. From the time of Harald Fairhair until the middle of the 13th century we know the names of skalds who served the kings of Norway. There is a peculiar development as to the recruitment of these skalds. Whereas most of the 9th and some of the 10th century poets seem to have been Norwegian, from about the year 1000 the Icelanders obtained a virtual monopoly of this profession at the royal Norwegian court. But as recently stated by two English historians of the Vikings: "This does not mean that Norwegians stopped making and appreciating scaldic composition, but it does mean that their work is not preserved in the twelfth- and

Banquet-scene from the Bayeux Tapestry.

thirteenth-century histories of the kings of Norway, almost all written by Icelanders, where much of the scaldic verse is to be found."*)

A skald might find fame and grow rich by attaching himself to a king's household. His poems are composed in special metres, and the skaldic diction is characterized by rare words, never used in everyday speech—*heiti,* and periphrastic expressions known as *kenningar* ('kennings'). Most of the skaldic verse composed at the royal court consists of poems in praise of the king and his dynasty. Quite often such a poem was composed after a king's death and recited to the deceased king's son and members of the royal family as a kind of obituary (an *erfidrápa*—a memo-

*) P. Foote & D. M. Wilson: The Viking Achievement (1970), p. 360.

rial poem). But generally speaking the skald's main task was to give his comments on a living king's deeds and character. The famous hirð-skald of Olav the Saint, Sigvat Thordsson, introduced himself to the king in the following verses:

> "Sinker of dark-blue ocean's steeds!
> Allow one scald to sing thy deeds;
> And listen to the song of one
> Who can sing well, if any can.
> For should the king despise all others,
> And show no favour to my brothers
> In scaldic art, yet all the same
> I still shall sing our great king's fame."

King Olav rewarded Sigvat with a gold ring weighing half a mark, and the Icelander was made one of the king's *hirðmenn*. Sigvat's spontaneous reply was as follows:

> "I willingly receive this sword—
> By land or sea, on shore, on board,
> I trust that I shall ever be
> Worthy the sword received from thee.
> A faithful follower thou hast bound—
> A generous master I have found;
> Master and servant both have made
> Just what best suits them by this trade."*)

The attendants of the Viking kings of Norway were sometimes skilled in the shaping of wood as well as of words.—At the court of the petty king of Vestfold at the beginning of the 9th century there seems to have been a team of wood-carvers at work, who have left rich evidence of their art in the Oseberg ship-grave finds. This exceptional wealth of wood-carving has left to posterity detailed information about the art of the period. The ship, a chariot, some sledges, a few animal-head posts, and some other objects have decorations in different styles. One artist, for instance, employs exactly the same motifs as are found

---

*) Translation by S. Laing and J. Simpson, 'Heimskringla', The Olaf Sagas, Part I (Everyman's Library) (1964), p. 148.

An animal head-post from the Oseberg ship. (Universitetets Oldsaksamling, Oslo.)

on certain bridle-mounts from Broa, Halla, in Gotland. Impressive decorations in this style are to be found on the stem and stern of the ship itself—interlocking animals deeply carved into the oak boards. Another artist, the so-called 'Academician', has created splendid decorations on a sledge-pole and on an animal-head post. The ceremonial chariot has a variety of ornaments. In one of the panels we may probably discern a motif from the popular legend of Gunnar in the snake pit.

The exquisite and time-consuming art of the Oseberg craftsmen bears sufficient witness to the cultural prominence of the Vestfold kings in the 9th century. The Oseberg burial mound, however, has also preserved remnants of tapestries, probably illustrating processions of a religious character. One of the main questions in the study of the pagan Scandinavian religion is that of the part which kings (or chieftains) are likely to have played in it. Was the king supposed by his people to be sacred, or did they only allow him the position of mediator between god and man? Neither contemporaries nor modern historians would find it easy to draw a clear line between a king of sacred nature and a king possessing the faculty of a divine mediator. It is quite evident, however, that most people regarded the king as a man apart and one possessing rare qualities. His dynasty was often traced back to some god, as in the case of Harald Fairhair; since he was supposed to be of the Yngling stock, the ancestors of this first king of Norway were traced back to the god Yngvi Frey. The king was thought to have some sort of communication with the fecundity gods. His popularity among the people depended on whether he was capable of securing the necessary conditions for a good crop. Harald Fairhair's father, Halvdan the Black, must have had excellent relations with the fertility gods: after his death his body was quartered, so that each of his main provinces might have a share.

As the kings of Norway played a leading part in introducing Christianity into Norway, it was only natural that the king became the virtual head of the Norwegian church during its first century of existence and until the foundation of the Nidaros (Trondheim) archiepiscopal see in 1153. This dominant royal position in the Norwegian Church also had a very real basis in the hailing of the Viking King Olav Haraldsson as a saint.

But both the pagan religion and Christianity were not the sole concern of kings; the religion of the people was also discussed at the local assemblies or *things*. There seems to have been a deep-rooted tradition that religion was intimately connected with justice and law.

At the local assembly or thing.

Important official functions in Viking society such as jurisdiction and legislation were performed by free men, assembled at local centres for a short spell of time during the summer. These local assemblies were called *things* (possibly meaning 'gatherings'), and the places where such assemblies met were considered sacred. Hence the 'thingstead' was enclosed by holy ropes, *vébǫnd*. A provision for fencing-in the 'thingstead' has been preserved in the older Law of the *Frostathing:* "It is an-

The procession from the Oseberg Tapestry. Reconstruction by Mary Storm. (Universitetets Oldsaksamling, Oslo.)

cient law that a bailiff (*ármaðr*) from each of the various shires shall set up an enclosure (*vébǫnd*) here at the *thingstead*. And the enclosure shall have sufficient space so that all who are appointed to the law court shall have ample room to sit within it." The *thing* referred to here is of the so-called *law-thing* (*lǫgþing*) type. These were provincial assemblies with appointed representatives, embracing most of Norway: the *Frostathing* covered Tröndelag and North Norway, the *Gulathing* western and southern Norway, the *Eidsivathing* the interior southeastern districts of Norway. Within these law provinces and also outside them there was a great variety of lesser district *things*, which all free men were expected to attend. All kinds of judicial matters were dealt with at the lesser local assemblies, and originally this judicial activity must have left some sort of case law, later to be incorporated into the old provincial laws. Any free man or woman could summon a *thing* when there was need; and a *thing* was summoned by sending out a stick or an arrow to be carried from farm to farm until the whole district had received the summons.

There is a rich tradition in the sagas and old Norse laws about the sessions and activities of the law *things*. In the saga of the skald and Viking Egil Skallagrimsson we get a strong impression that the presence of sheer force might influence the proceedings of a *thing*. Egil Skallagrimsson, having married a daughter of the chieftain Björn Brynjolvsson of Aurland, Sogn, demanded on behalf of his wife a share in the inheritance after her father. But the chieftain Berg-Onund, married to another of Björn's daughters, had taken possession of all the property owned by Björn and refused to give up any of it to Egil's wife, Asgjerd. The saga-writer then goes on to say: "Egil saw that Onund would do no right in this matter, then he summoned him to court, and referred the matter to the law of the Gula-thing." In the ensuing dispute between the two men it turns out that Berg-Onund has a reliable friend in the king of Norway, Eric Bloodaxe, whereas Egil has a wise supporter and staunch friend in the chieftain Arinbjörn. "The winter wore away, and the time came when men should go to the Gula-thing. Arinbjörn took to the king a numerous company, among them went Egil. King Eric was there, numerously attended. Berg-Onund was among his train, as were his brothers; there was a large following. But when the meeting was to be held about men's lawsuits, both parties went where the court was set, to plead their proofs. Then was Onund full of big words. Now where the court sat, there was a level plot with hazel-poles planted in a ring and with twisted ropes around [and between] the poles [thus encircling the plot]. This was called *vébǫnd* (holy ropes). Within the ring sat twelve judges of the Firðafylki, twelve of the Sygnafylki, and twelve of the Hǫrðafylki. These three twelves of men were to declare the law in all the suits. Arinbjörn ruled who should be judges from the Firðafylki, Tord of Aurland who should be so from the Sygnafylki. All these were of one party. Arinbjörn had brought to the *thing* a long-ship fully equipped, also many small craft and store-ships. King Eric had six or seven long-ships all well equipped. A great many farmers (yeomen) were also there.

Egil began to plead thus: He requested the judges to give him lawful judgment in the suit between him and Onund. He then set forth what proofs he held on his claim on the property that had belonged to Björn Brynjolvsson. He said that Asgjerd, daughter of Björn, his own wife, was rightful heiress, *oðal*-born, of landed gentry, and of titled family further back. He demanded that the judges should adjudge to Asgjerd half of Björn's inheritance, land as well as chattels."

After Egil had spoken, Onund began to speak in his own defence. His argumentation was chiefly to the effect that Asgjerd had no *legal* right to her father's property, as she was born after her parents had eloped from Norway and were outlawed. And Onund termed Asgjerd the king's 'bondwoman' as she "was begotten when her father and mother were outlawed by the king".

Arinbjörn became furious at Onund's words, especially at Onund's reference to Asgjerd as the king's 'bondwoman'. He stood up and began to speak: "Evidence we will bring, King Eric, in this case, and oaths we will add, that this was expressly provided in the reconciliation between my father and Björn Hold [Brynjolvsson], that Asgjerd, daughter of Björn and Tora [Arinbjörn's sister] was to have right of inheritance after Björn her father; and this in addition, which you know full well, O King, that you restored Björn to his rights in Norway,....." To these words the King found no ready answer. ..... Then Arinbjörn produced witnesses, twelve men, and all well chosen. These men had all been present and heard the reconciliation between Tore and Björn, and they offered to the king and judges to swear to it. The judges were willing to accept their oath if the King did not forbid it."

Then Gunhild, King Eric's queen, intervened. She hated Egil Skallagrimsson and would not tolerate that Onund was 'trodden under foot' by Egil. She urged her brother Alv to 'persuade' the judges not to give the wrong judgment. Alv and his men went to the court-enclosure, and "cut to pieces the *vébǫnd* and tore down the poles, and then scattered the judges. There was great uproar in the *thing*, but all men there were weaponless.

Then spoke Egil: 'Can Berg-Onund hear my words?' 'I hear', said Onund. 'Then I do challenge you to combat, and be our fight here at the *thing*. Let whoever of us two wins the victory have this property, both lands and chattels.' — — —

Whereupon King Eric made this answer: 'If you, Egil, are strongly bent on fighting, then we will grant you this forthwith'. Egil replied: 'I will not fight against you or an overwhelming force; but before equal numbers I will not flee, if this be given me. Nor will I then make any distinction of persons, titled or untitled.'

Arinbjørn then spoke: 'Let us go away, Egil. We shall not here effect today anything that will be to our gain'. And with this Arinbjörn and all his people turned to depart."

Although the saga of Egil Skallagrimsson is preserved in manuscripts from the 13th and 14th centuries only, so that we must assume that it reflects to some extent conditions of the 13th century, the general atmosphere is that of the restless Viking age. The episode at the *Gulathing* presented above throws light on a time when social disputes were not always decided by legal procedure, but by force. It also sheds light on a period when the conflict between the new royal power over Norway and traditional local authority, vested in the chieftains, was still undecided.

Such legal institutions as the *things* were to be found throughout the lands and islands settled by Norse Vikings: in Ireland, in the Isle of Man, in Northumbria, in the Hebrides, in Caithness, in the Orkneys, in Shetland, in the Faeroes, in Iceland, and in Greenland. With the establishment of *things* better conditions were provided for the introduction of law and peaceful settlement of feuds and disputes instead of having recourse to violence and bloodshed. With the support of royal and chieftain authority the law of the land gradually prevailed over the general lawlessness of the Viking period. A further strengthening of the reign of law came with the introduction of Christianity, with its special demand on the individual and with its own set of provisions for the violation of the law of God. Viking raids and Viking plundering were not permitted by the Christian church, the Christian kings of Scandinavia, and the provincial *things,* jointly controlled by king and bishop. The Gulathing Law contains this illuminating provision, which probably dates from the 11th century or earlier: "If a man builds a long-ship out on the countryside, but makes no announcement as to his plans or whither he intends to sail, then the bailiff *(ármaðr)* or the sheriff *(lendrmaðr)* shall go to him and ask whither he intends to sail. If he refuses to tell, they shall demand that he give bail to the amount of forty marks. But if he refuses to give bail, they shall cut out a board five ells in length on either side of the keel. If they fail to do this, the farmers shall do it and also remove the sail, if there is one, and in this way prevent the sailing. But if they fail to do this, and the ship turns out to be a warship, they shall pay a mark for every thwart and three marks for the rudder strap; that is called thwart money."*)

*) Quoted from L. M. Larson, ed.: *The earliest Norwegian Laws* (1935), p. 198.

IV. NORSEMEN IN WESTERN EUROPE AND THE NORTH ATLANTIC REGION

Modern Scandinavian historians look upon the Viking expansion in the Baltic coastal area and Russia as a creation of settlements within rather limited areas. It seems to have been the aim of the Vikings to capture strategically important places along the rivers and main trading routes of eastern Europe, in order to bring under their control the profitable trade between the Orient and western Europe. We know today that the Swedish or Rus expansion in the Baltic started in the pre-Viking period, but it is still true to say that a large-scale penetration of the vast Russian plains along the rivers only began in the 9th century. How soon did the traders from Scandinavia, and primarily Sweden, play a predominant part in the trade between the east and the west, and how soon did the effects of this intercontinental trade make itself felt in Scandinavia? Is it possible to point to a direct relationship between the Oriental trade of the Swedes, the assumed prosperity of Scandinavia, and the Viking expeditions to the west? The Swedish professor, Sture Bolin, to whom we have previously referred, had no doubt about an early Swedish expansion in Russia and an early Swedish predominance in its trade. As a corollary of this, he saw a connection between the Oriental trade and silver and the expeditions to the west.

But is it possible in the case of Norway to accept this general thesis as the principal explanation of Viking expansion from this part of Scandinavia? In order to find out something about the causes of economic growth in Norway during the Viking period, we propose to analyse the forms of activity in various Viking territories abroad as well as in the mother country. Only then can we go on to ask which activity was predominant in a particular area, and why Norsemen were engaged in such an activity there at a given time. Eventually we will try to compare

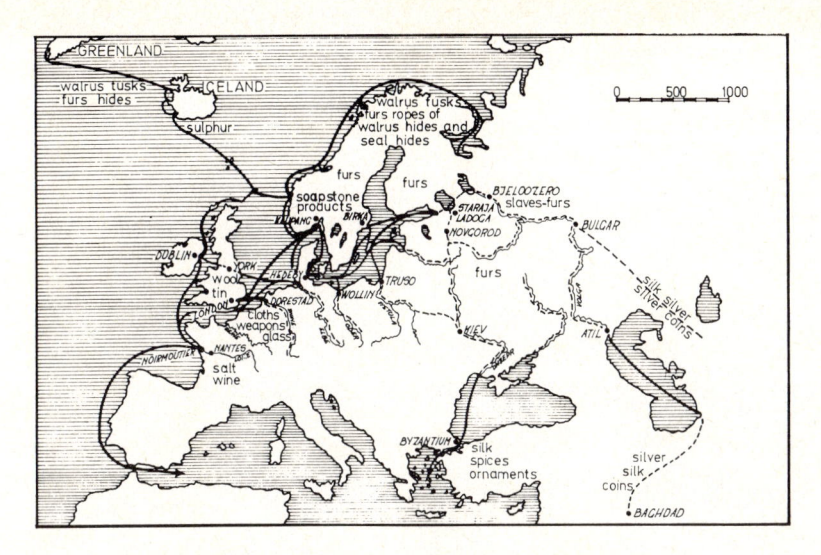

Principal trading routes of the Vikings — main commodities. (Distance in kilometers.)

forms of Viking activity abroad and at home in order to shed light on the Norwegian background of the expeditions to the west.

The British Isles.

The British Isles were undoubtedly the main theatre of operations for the Vikings coming from Norway. We know now that they settled in the northern isles of Scotland, in Caithness, Sutherland, the coastal districts of western mainland Scotland, in the Inner and Outer Hebrides and the Isle of Man, in Ireland, southwestern Wales, and in the northwestern and northeastern parts of England.

In earlier Norwegian historical writing it was common to explain the first settlements in Iceland, the Faeroes, and the British Isles as a result of the political unification of Norway by king Harald Fairhair towards the end of the 9th century. Recent British and Norwegian archaeological and toponymical research has shown, however, that the Norse invasion and land-taking in the British and North Atlantic islands must have begun before king Harald's final conquest of Norway.

The bishop's church at the Brough of Birsay, Orkney, together with ruins of the earl's palace and a cluster of Norse longhouse-sites. In the background Main-land. (Photo Professor Emeritus Gordon Donaldson, University of Edinburgh.)

Shetland and **Orkney** were among the first island groups to be visited by the Vikings. The *Orkneyinga Saga* has no explanation as to why the Norsemen went out to these islands. In the *Historia Norwegiae* (The Panmure Codex) there is a description of how the Norse settlers had to fight the Picts in Orkney before they won the islands. To judge from archaeological and toponymical research by British and Norwegian experts there are few indications of a dramatic clash between the men of the East and the Picts in the islands of Orkney and Shetland. Consequently it is not very likely that the Norsemen came to these island-groups just to harry and plunder. Relatively recent excavations of dwelling sites at Underhoull and Jarlshof (Shetland) and at the Brough of Birsay, Deerness, Buckquoy, Tuquoy and Westness (Orkney) have brought to light Norse types of houses. More or less occasional grave finds such as the Pierowall finds of the 9th and 10th centuries correspond very well with the general Norwegian pattern. But the most convincing source material is undoubtedly the place-names in general and the farm-names in particular. Although the late Orkney scholar

Isle of Man scenery. Tynwald Hill and St. John's Church. In the background Beary Mountain and Lammel (Old Norse: Lambafiall) (Copyright Aftenposten.)

Hugh Marwick may probably be exaggerating when he considers 99% of the farm-names to be of Norse origin, the percentage is sufficient to substantiate a massive land-taking by the Norse. The distribution and number of farm-names ending in *-staðir, boer, -land,* and *-bólstaðr* seem to indicate an early culmination of immigration; its peak was probably before the middle of the 9th century. There can be little doubt about the fact that the bulk of the Norse settlers in Shetland and Orkney came there to find new land–pastures and tillable soil. At the same time we should hesitate to exclude other motives. The densely populated places of Pierowall and Birsay may probably have served as Viking bases and trading stations besides being regional centres of the farm community.

We know less about the Norse settlements in *Caithness* and *the Hebrides.* But place names and archaeological finds seem to point in the same direction as in Orkney and Shetland. There must have been a large-scale invasion of Norse farmers in search of fertile land. The settlement must have occurred somewhat later.

The first settling of *the Isle of Man,* to judge from grave

71

finds, seems to have begun about the middle of the 9th century. In this small island, however, the Norsemen came across a well-established Celtic population which was able to hold its own against the Viking invaders; this resulted in the blending of races and a composite culture. Outstanding monuments to Hiberno-Norse collaboration are the runic crosses (see p. 13) and certain features of the Manx social organization.—The backbone of the island's economy in the Viking period was undoubtedly agriculture. But its strategical position in the Irish Sea on one of the main trading routes, attracted foreign merchants and pirates alike. Hence it is more difficult to decide which was the main inducement to Norse Vikings. It is probably safe to say that both trade and agriculture were important activities among the Norsemen who had settled in the Isle of Man.

The Viking invasion of *Ireland* began as raids at the beginning of the 9th century. It was directed against the coasts and offshore islands. The invaders were almost certainly both from Norway and the Scottish isles where the Vikings had already established bases: Shetland, Orkney, and the Hebrides. Real settlement, however, hardly started until the 830's. In the early 840's the Irish annals contain references to foreign settlements at Dublin, Wexford, Waterford, Cork and Limerick. Around 850 the Norse invaders and settlers had to fight on two fronts—against the Irish and against Danish Vikings coming over from England. The outcome seems to have been that the Norse settlers stood their ground and fastened their grip on the ports just mentioned. Fortifications were built around them. Under the leadership of Olav the White and other Viking chieftains the Norsemen were able to organize petty kingdoms in Ireland, the most important of which, Dublin, managed to retain some independence until Strongbow, the Earl of Pembroke, and his Anglo-Normans came over about 1170. A slow but constant mingling of Irish and Norse began in the 9th century, and the purely Norse character of the settlements soon began to disappear.

Was the basic economy of the Norse settlements in Ireland the same as in Orkney and Shetland? Three facts should be emphasized in reply to this question: The colonies were built

Excavations of Irish-Norse Dublin at the Cathedral. (Copyright Aftenposten.)

on estuaries, or at the bottom of fjords; they soon became cores of towns; and their agrarian character was never very marked. There is general agreement among historians that the main basis of subsistence for the men from the east, the *lochlannaighs,* was trade and craftsmanship, and not the tilling of soil. The men of Dublin and other Norse towns traded with the Irish farmers and with countries like France, England and Norway. The sources for such general conclusions are the Irish annals, the relatively few archaeological finds, chiefly concentrated in the city of Dublin, and the rather scanty place-name material from the coastal areas.

The phases of Scandinavian activity in *England* seem fairly well established. Raids by smaller bands of Vikings along the coasts in the decades before and after 800 were followed by the organization of these bands into greater units about the middle of the century (in the Anglo-Saxon Chronicle mentioned as *here* or *micel here*). In 867 the Vikings captured York, and they gradually settled down in the land. In 876 the Anglo-Saxon Chronicle (E-version) reports that Halvdan "shared out the lands of Northumbria, and they were engaged in ploughing and in making a living for themselves". The great land-taking had begun, and it was completed throughout most of northeastern England before the end of the 9th century, although we cannot exclude the likelihood that there were reinforcements from home and other Viking colonies in the 10th century and later. The Danelaw was established to the northeast of Watling Street, the old Roman road between London and Chester; and Northumbria was organized as a Viking petty kingdom in cooperation with the Archbishop of York. Although York during the Viking age became an important centre of commerce, the predominant character of the Danish settlement was agrarian. An engaging discussion is going on among historians, archaeologists and place-name scholars as to the extent and organizational pattern of the Danish land-taking. And place-names have played a great part in the debate, especially place-name compounds ending in *-by* (Danby, Whitby, Derby, etc.). The majority of the Danish scholars look upon the Scandinavian place-names in general and the *-by*-names in particular as definite evidence of a large-scale Danish invasion of settlers in northeastern England, while a group of British historians rejects the Danish thesis on the basis of few archaeological finds and their evaluation of the Anglo-Danish place-name material. The English historian P. H. Sawyer has formulated important principles for the use of place-name material, which provide the core of the argumentation against the Danish mass-immigration theory: "The study of place-names can reveal something of the origin of the settlers, and it can indicate . . . where those settlements were. It cannot define the exact extent of the first settlements any more than it can reveal the number of settlers . . .".

Norsemen as well as Danes took part in the settlement of northern England during the Viking period. Place-name scholars and historians have been able to locate the Norse settlements in South Wales, Yorkshire, Northumberland, Cheshire, Lancashire, Westmorland and Cumberland. The Norsemen moved from north to south and west to east; very few of them came directly from Norway. According to the Yorkshire historian A. L. Binns they began to arrive in Northumbria shortly after 900. And he considers that as an immigration group it differs from the earlier Danish settlers "by the strength of its paganism, its connection with Celtic lands and the strength of its Norwegian element". The Norsemen coming from the west, however, were deeply influenced by their previous stay in Ireland. Hence their major contribution to the culture of the Viking kingdom of Northumbria, in Mr. Binns' opinion, "was Irish and Norwegian".

Why did the Norsemen who had originally settled in Ireland and the Isle of Man, and later in northwestern England, go into Northumbria? Their forms of settlement and the places in which they settled give some answer to this question. Their settlements are to be found along the river routes penetrating the Pennines from the west to the east, and leading to such important centres as York and the mouth of the Tyne, thus opening up overland trading routes between the Irish and the North Sea. But by themselves these valley settlements to the east of the Pennines do not entitle us to draw any conclusions as to the main motives of the Norse immigrants. It is essential to know something about their land-taking and activities and the time of their arrival in northwestern England, in order to shed more light on the invasion of Northumbria.

The raids against the coasts of Cumberland and Lancashire began about the middle of the 9th century, but the phase of actual land-taking did not occur before the first quarter of the 10th century (according to E. Ekwall, the Anglo-Swedish place-name scholar). There is no doubt about the mixed origin of the immigrants. Their sculptured stones and crosses have Celtic affinities, their churches were dedicated to Celtic saints (St. Patrick, St. Bridget and St. Columba), and their place-names

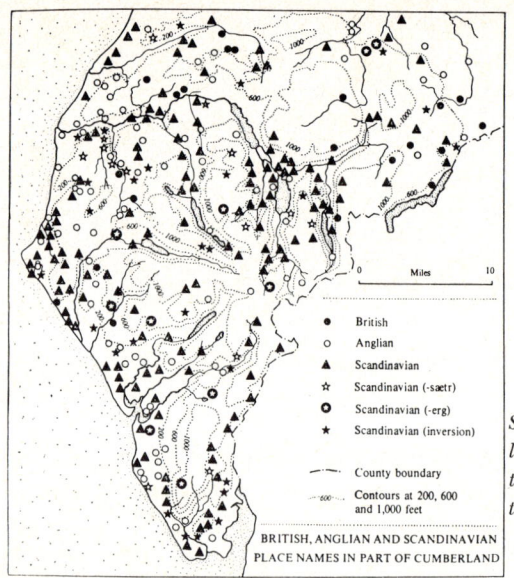

Settlement map of Cumberland. (W. Rollinson, A History of Man in the Lake District (1967), p. 59.)

were often inversion compounds in the Celtic fashion, many of them also containing the element *erg* (<Gaelic *airge*), which means a shieling or summer pasture farm. The density of Norse place-names, especially in Cumberland, but also in the neighbouring districts of Westmorland and Lancashire, makes it quite clear that the majority of the Norsemen here had come to find new land, both tillable soil and pastures. At the same time we cannot exclude the idea of a centrally directed immigration policy on the part of the Norse-Irish kings of Dublin, who in the first half of the 10th century invaded Northumbria and became kings of York. At the middle of the century they were replaced by a Norwegian prince, who came more or less directly from his homeland—Eric Bloodaxe, the son and dethroned successor of Harald Fairhair, the unifying king of Norway. With Eric the first main phase of the Viking movement came to an end. In the second and final one the rulers of the more or less unified realms of Scandinavia and England clashed in battles for empire.

The Frankish Empire—Normandy.
According to the Anglo-Saxon Chronicle the invasion of *Normandy* by Rollo (Rolf) and his Vikings began in 876, the very same year as Halvdan "shared out the lands of Northumbria" among his men. But the attacks on the *Frankish Empire* had started much earlier. In 834 the Frisian town of Dorestad was sacked and burnt by Danish Vikings. About 840 the Viking attacks had reached the coasts of the English Channel. In 845 they harried Paris and put to flight the levies of King Charles the Bald.—The Vikings raiding the Frankish Empire were usually termed Normans by contemporary Frankish annalists. However, at times other names were used. Those Normans who attacked and captured Nantes in 843 were given a special name by the local Frankish annalist—*Westfaldingi,* which by most historians has been interpreted as "men from Vestfold". In other words the leading men and possibly the majority of the men in this Viking fleet must have had their homes in the districts to the west of the Oslofjord, the region from which the unification of Norway started some thirty or forty years later. If the interpretation of the *Westfaldingi*-name is correct, and if the saga tradition of Rollo's or Rolf's family connection with the Norwegian Earls of Möre is reliable (and most modern British, French and Norwegian historians think it is), then it can be said that Vikings from Norway also played an important part in the invasion of this area of western Europe, sharing in the early attacks and showing their interest not only in piracy and booty, but also in trade. The *Westfaldingi* after Nantes returned with a huge booty to the island of Noirmoutier off the Loire estuary, the island being an important international market for the trade in wine and salt. And Vikings stayed there in their fortified camp every winter until 890, benefiting from the profits of the market trade, constantly being reinforced from Norse Ireland, the Danelaw and other parts of France.

Although the Danes certainly played the major part in the conquest and formation of the Norman state in Normandy, it is reasonable to conclude that some of Rollo's retainers at least were of Norse stock. Thus the place-name material from the Cotentin peninsula seems to document a relatively strong Norse-Irish population element in this area.

Ile de Noirmoutier: a traditional product of the island —salt. (Photo Jacques Boulas.)

The Isles and Lands of the North Atlantic.
The Norse immigration into the islands along the coasts of western Europe was chiefly marked by its violent character. The invaders had to fight against an earlier population. This was not the case in the islands of the Faeroes, Iceland and Greenland, where the Norse settlers came to areas that had little or no population. Hence the land-taking in these islands was mainly peaceful.

According to the Færeyinga Saga *the Faroes* were settled during the reign of king Harald Fairhair (i.e. in the fourth quarter of the 9th century and the first of the 10th). In his work *De mensura orbis terrae*, written about 825, the Irish monk Dicuil mentions some distant islands in the Atlantic, where a few Irish *papas* had recently been driven out by Norse pirates. It seems highly probable that he is referring to the Faroe islands. However, neither archaeological finds nor the place-names of the islands have so far given us the clue to the dating of the Norse immigration into the Faroes. It is reasonable to conclude, however, that it must have taken place shortly before or at the same time as the settlement of Iceland, and that the

Kirkjubœr, the religious centre of Norse Færoes. (Copyright Aftenposten.)

main invasion must have occurred in the second part of the 9th century.

Ari froði's Book of the Icelanders *(Íslendingabók)*, written about 1125, and The Book of the Land-taking *(Landnámabók)*, the shorter original version of which was probably written at the same time, possibly by Ari himself, give us good information about the Viking settlement of *Iceland*. Most of the land-taking was completed between 870 and 930. We also know how the emigration from Norway and from the Norse colonies in the British Isles was organized. It was a massive westward movement of farmers and fishermen, mostly from western Norway, and led by chieftains who possessed sufficient resources to build the big ships necessary to bring along their household and their dependents. We may safely assume that the settlement in Iceland had an aristocratic character. We are not going to discuss here the motives which caused people from Norway to brave the dangers of a long Atlantic crossing; suffice it to be said that about 6000 people left for Iceland in the course of sixty years.

Greenland was not settled directly from Norway, although the leader of the first immigration party was born there.

Þingvellir. The plains of the thing or law assembly of all Icelanders. (Photo Páll Jónsson.)

Eirik the Red had come with his father Thorvald to Iceland and was outlawed there for several murders about 985. He went across the sea to the snow-covered land in the northwest and explored parts of its east and west coasts. On the west coast he came to fjords without ice and therefore thought it proper to call this land *Greenland*. He went back to Iceland and told people about the juicy grass and the rich fauna along the Greenland fjords. And a year later he led a fleet of about 25 ships of immigrants to the new land. The colony prospered, and in its best period during the 13th century numbered about 300 farms and probably between 1800 and 2100 people. The means of subsistence for the Norse Greenlanders were pasture-farming, fishing, and hunting. The settlement could not exist without trade, without selling such products as walrus-tusks, hides, furs, and possibly dried fish, and without buying such commodities as grain, timber, and iron.

The voyages from Iceland and Greenland to distant coasts in the west were milestones in the history of exploration. There can

Brattahlið. The farm of Eric the Red in the Eastern Settlement, Greenland. (Copyright Aftenposten.)

be no doubt about the fact that men from Iceland found *Vinland* (or North America). But from the point of view of settlement the expeditions and attempts at land-taking were no more than just episodes. The dwelling sites which Helge Ingstad has found and excavated together with his wife at L'Anse-aux-Meadows in Newfoundland cannot be taken to prove anything but a short-lived attempt by some settlers to stay there in the Middle Ages. According to the saga tradition the most daring of all Norse settlements turned out a failure. Thorfinn Karlsevni and his followers had to return to Greenland.

It is not very difficult to ascertain which forms of activity were predominant in the various regions invaded by the Vikings. Raiding and war have more often than not prepared the ground for some sort of settlement. In some areas the Norse invaders wanted land for agriculture and pasture-farming, in other regions they seem to have been more interested in trade. The tasks facing the historian who wants to throw light on the causes of

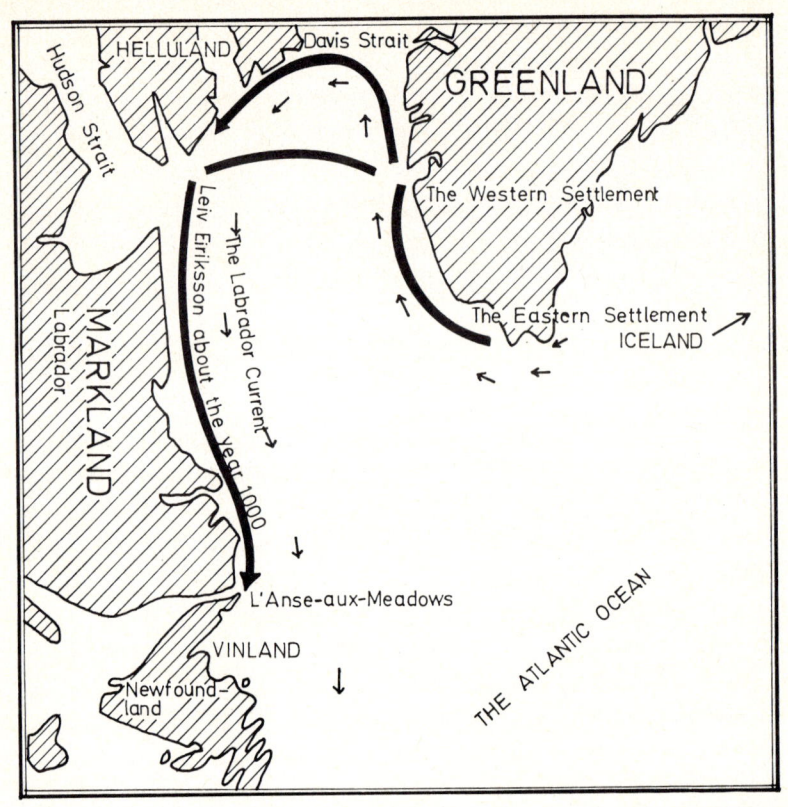

The discovery of America. Anne Stine and Helge Ingstad's excavations at L'Anse-aux-Meadows have thrown new light on the expeditions of the Norsemen to the east coast of the American continent.

Viking immigration into a territory overseas, are first to establish the conditions in the area in question previous to the Viking invasion; then the main occupation of the settlers during the settlement process, together with the dating of this process; and finally the local Scandinavian origin of the newcomers. This again will necessitate a shifting of the historian's focus from events and conditions in the Viking colonies to the activities going on at the same time at home. The juxtaposition and comparison of the Norse movement abroad and at home may enable us to understand more clearly why people from Norway went out to distant coasts in western Europe and across the North Atlantic.

Let us briefly summarize the main phases of the Norse Viking settlement abroad.—In *the British Isles* all three main forms of activity are represented (war, land-taking and trade), but not at the same time in the different areas concerned. The Norse settlement in *Shetland* and *Orkney* took place mostly during the 9th century, with immigration culminating in the first half of the century. The sparse population of Irish monks and Picts was driven out or subdued, probably without much violence. Agricultural pursuits, fishing and pasture farming took most of the time for these settlers, but we cannot exclude raiding along the coasts of the Irish Sea and trading with Dublin and Norway and even more distant parts of Europe.—In *Caithness* and *the Hebrides* we find a repetition of the process under the same conditions at a slightly later date, possibly in the second half of the 9th century and the first half of the tenth.—The settlement of the *Isle of Man* must be dated to the second half of the 9th century, although Norse immigrants seem to have arrived in great numbers during the following century as well. We do not possess much evidence of a native Manx commerce, but it is reasonable to conclude that trade with other markets played as important a part for the Norsemen on the island as agriculture and fishing.—In *Ireland* the settlement took on a definite commercial character after a protracted period of fighting against the Irish during most of the 9th century. The Norse settlements were concentrated at estuaries, fjords and fortified towns (Dublin, Carlingford, Waterford, Wexford, Cork, and Limerick). The Norsemen here formed urban communities in strategic areas just like the Swedes in Russia.—In *England* both the Danish and Norse settlement started relatively late after almost a century of raiding and warfare, first in smaller bands, then in greater units ('hosts'). Between 876 and 900 the Danish land-taking took place in eastern England from East Anglia in the south to Northumberland in the north. Place-name evidence establishes a relatively large-scale immigration. The Norse settlement in northern England came mostly from Galloway, Norse Dublin, the Hebrides and the Isle of Man and contributed a predominantly Norse population to Cumberland and parts of Westmorland, Lancashire, the Wirral peninsula of Cheshire, and South Wales during the period round 900. During the first half of the 10th century the Norse settlers crossed the Pennines into the former counties of Northumberland and Yorkshire. Whereas land-taking most certainly was the prime motive in the Norse settlement of the northwest, trade cannot be excluded as an important driving-force behind the continued expansion into Northeast England.

After the death of Charlemagne (814) *the Frankish Empire* was disintegrating, and its long, more or less undefended coasts were open to Viking attacks. Hence the Vikings here seem to have preferred raiding for booty to other activities for a longer period than in any other Viking-infested region. But here also trade seems to go hand in hand with war, as is strongly suggested by the long Viking control of the profitable salt and wine market on the Noirmoutier island off the Loire estuary. The land-taking phase set in about 900, and the settlement was concentrated upon the coastal area between the rivers Sélune and Bresle on both sides of the Seine estuary and also in the Cotentin peninsula.

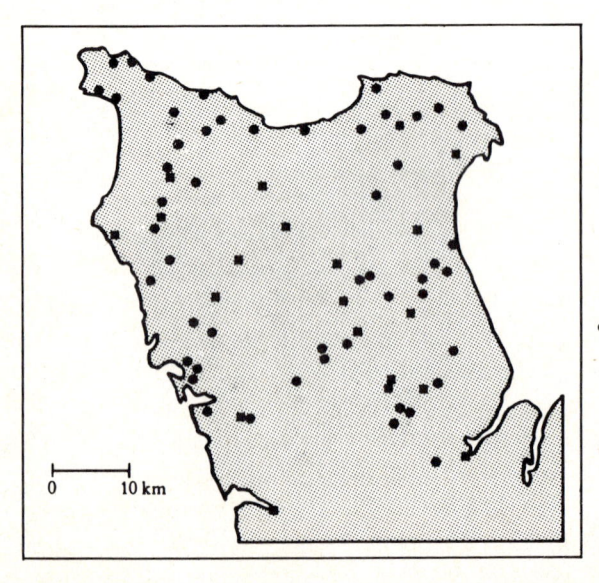

Scandinavian place-names in the Contentin (material from Adigard des Gautries, Noms de personnes scandinaves).

• Place-names combining a Scandinavian personal name and a Frankish suffix

■ Other names containing Scandinavian elements (usually entirely Scandinavian)

After a treaty with King Charles the Simple in 911 Rollo with the support of his followers changed their land of conquest into a and the immigrants undoubtedly came chiefly from Denmark and from the Danish settlements in England, but a smaller element of the settlers certainly came from Norway and Norse Ireland.

We have mentioned that the land-taking on the islands of the North Atlantic – the Faroes, Iceland and Greenland – took place relatively late: *The Faroes* were settled during the second half of the 9th century, Iceland from 870 to 930. *Greenland* from 986 onwards. The Norsemen and the Norse-Irish going out to these distant lands, were probably first and foremost seeking new land, but we shall not overemphasize the need for tillable soil. Pasture farming, fishing, and hunting were even more important activities than agriculture. Hence trade with Norway and Europe in general was an important part of the life of the Faroese, the Icelanders, and the Greenlanders. The immigration into the North Atlantic islands was first and foremost a mass emigration from Norway. Why did it occur between 850 and 1000? Why did the invasion of the British Isles take place earlier? Only a careful survey of conditions in Norway during the 8th, 9th and 10th centuries can throw more light on the causes of the Norse expansion overseas.

V. THE NORWEGIAN BACKGROUND IN ITS SCANDINAVIAN AND EUROPEAN CONTEXT

It has been a main question in earlier Norwegian (and Scandinavian) research whether the Viking expansion overseas was due to overpopulation at home. The explanations given had more or less the character of guesswork, and quite naturally so. The sagas and skaldic poems were insufficient sources for estimating the growth of population during the Viking age and the preceding centuries. Between the two World Wars and especially after 1945 the study of the Viking period has gradually attracted a considerable body of scholars from the fields of archaeology, place-name studies and history, and their interest is not directed towards the sagas and the skaldic poems in the first place, but towards quantitative material such as farm names and archaeological finds. Local historians have been able to give more penetrating accounts of the local pre-historic and Viking development of a region, partly by a recording of all the settlement names in their topographical situation and partly by distributing these names, and especially farm names, among such chronological periods as the *Roman period* (first four centuries A.D.), *the Migration period* (400–600), *the Merovingian period* (600–800), *the Viking age,* and *the Christian Middle ages.* Then the results of these investigations are compared with recorded archaeological finds from the same region. The correlation between these two groups of source material may, as a rule, give some indication of the population development and expansion or contraction of settlement in the locality in question.

On the basis of recent farm-name research in Norway it is permissible to propound as a thesis that Norway had a growing population in the Merovingian and Viking periods. We are interested in the causes of this growth and shall return to it below.—But contemporary with the population growth there seems to have been a constantly expanding commerce between

Norway (Scandinavia) and Europe. At the same time a brisk local trade was going on between the interior districts and the coastal areas.

The interior expansion in Norway therefore has two important aspects: a population growth with a resulting extension of the settled area, and an increase of domestic and foreign trade with such evident results as the formation of the first known markets and town-type centres at different places along the coast and in the interior. How did these two activities affect the Viking expeditions to the west?

Whereas Swedish and some Danish scholars studying the Viking period have been mainly concerned with the commercial expansion of Scandinavia, Norwegian historians have turned their attention chiefly to the problems of expanding settlement and overpopulation. This interest seems to have its roots in a strong Norwegian tradition of place-name research going back to the mid-19th century. The pioneers of the study of Norwegian place-names, P. A. Munch, Oluf Rygh and Magnus Olsen, introduced important principles of chronological and social classification of *farm names*.

In giving a brief survey of classes of farm names according to the system formulated primarily by Rygh and Olsen, we shall be concerned especially with compound names ending in *-vin, -heimr, -land, setr, -býr(-boer)* and *-staðir*. In addition to these there is a big group of farm names consisting of monosyllabic words taken from physical features like *nes, ås, aker* (i.e. naze, hill, field). According to Rygh and Olsen, farm-names from this group may be the oldest, possibly going back to the centuries before Christ's nativity – to the Celtic iron age or even to the Bronze age. The next group with names ending in *-vin* and *-heimr* may be dated back to the Roman period (defined above). During the Migration period new groups of compound names bacame popular in namegiving: *-land* and *-setr*-names. Finally we may mention three groups of farm-names which occur with marked frequency during the Merovingian and Viking periods, viz. those ending in *-staðir, -býr(-boer) -bólstaðr* and *-þveit*.

In the modern study of the growth of settlement in Norway during the Viking age it is primarily the *-staðir*-group of farm-names, with supporting archaeological material, which forms the basis for a general assumption that there was a considerable expansion of settlement and growth of population. The historian usually distinguishes between *-stadir*-names with a first element which is either obscure or connected with topography (such as *Blesa-staðir, Flagarstaðir,* and *Bliustaðir)* and compounds in which the first element is a personal name (as for instance, *Rolfstaðir, Herleifstaðir,* and *Ulfstaðir).* It is also usual to associate the latter group with the Viking period, while the former is regarded as older. In quite recent place-name research, however, new views have been propounded as to the absolute and relative chronology of the farm names. Scholars have become more hesitant in ascribing the different farm-name groups to definite periods. With regard to the *-staðir* group it is a tendency to look upon a proportion of the compounds, among others those with rare personal names, as pre-Viking.

In the region of Trøndelag it is quite safe to assume, on the basis of recent research, that most of the *-staðir* farms were settled during the Merovingian period. In the Viking period the less numerous *-setr*-names predominated there. In the Sognefjord area we find a similar development during these two periods. But as full studies of the farm-name material in this region are lacking, we can only base this assumption on a general impression of the *-staðir* and *-setr* farms as being relatively old dwellings from the pre-Viking period.

A great many *-land* and *-boer* farms may also be dated to the Merovingian period, although the majority of the *-land farms* were evidently taken up in the Migration period, while the great mass of *-boer* or *-býr* farms seems to have been settled in the Viking age.

The chief method employed in dating the *-staðir* farm-names as well as the other groups is archaeological, although the topographical approach which takes into account the situation and position of a farm in relation to the other farms of a certain district is just as essential. It goes without saying, however, that a student of farm-names feels rather reassured when he is able to date a certain farm by grave finds from the holding. But an archaeological find cannot automatically be connected with the

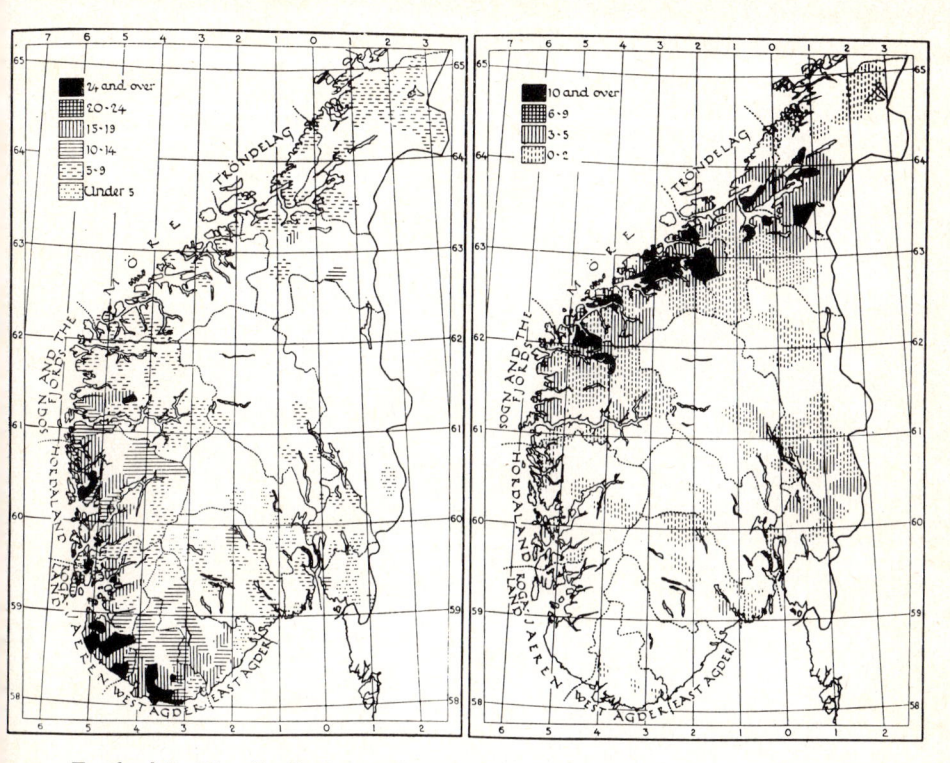

To the left: The distribution of -land place-names in Norway. (A.W. Brøgger, Ancient Emigrants (1929), plate facing p. 84).

To the right: The distribution of -setr place-names in Norway. (A.W. Brøgger, Ancient Emigrants (1929), plate facing p. 74.)

farm where the find has been made: the question always arises as to whether the find belonged to the same farm in the prehistoric periods. A few cautious conclusions may perhaps be drawn from recent farm-name research. On the basis of farm-name and archaeological material it must be correct to say that a strong growth of population and expansion of settlement began in the region of Trøndelag, parts of western Norway (especially the Möre, Sognefjord and Rogaland areas), and in southeastern Norway at the beginning of the 8th century. It probably reached a climax towards the end of the century. Then at about 900 there seems to have been a temporary contraction of settlement in Norway and possibly also a decline of population.

How shall we explain this course of events? One method of exploring it may be, or rather should be, to see the development of settlement in relation to the Norse expansion overseas. Do we find the same farm-name groups in such settlements as Orkney and Iceland? And if so, is there any correlation between the farm-names of the same classes?

In Orkney 23 -*staðir* names have been identified, 26 -*boer* names, 50 -*bólstaðr* -*names*, 35 *land* names, and 25 -*setr* names; in Iceland the corresponding figures are 1165 -*staðir* farms, 174 -*boer* farms, 11-*bólstaðr* farms, 77 -*land* farms, whereas no old -*setr* names are found. It is unimportant in this connection to go into the moot question of the social stratification of the various name-groups. It must be sufficient to say that the majority of the -*land* and -*setr* farms of Norway are considered secondary in relation to the -*staðir*, -*vin* and -*heimr* farms. It is fairly certain that the -*setr* farms in northwestern Norway, Tröndelag, and the upper parts of Gudbrandsdalen, Valdres, Hallingdal and Hedmark, and a great many of the -*land* farms of southwestern Norway reflect a settlement extension farther into the hinterland and also towards the outer coastal area. These farms, mostly on marginal land and much exposed to crop failure, would soon be deserted when better opportunities became available. The propitious time came in the 9th century.

The first waves of Viking emigration from Norway must undoubtedly be seen as an overpopulation phenomenon in the -*land* and -*setr* regions: i.e. primarily in the fjord regions of northwestern and southwestern Norway, where tillable soil and pasture land were scarce. The settlement of Orkney and Shetland, as the later settlement of Iceland, should therefore be looked upon as a continuation of a settlement movement which had begun inside Norway in the Merovingian period.

We have established population growth as one of the social forces explaining the Viking expeditions to the west. But why did this expansion overseas occur precisely in the 9th and 10th centuries? It is quite evident that population growth by itself only gives part of the background. A highly significant question

The Gokstad ship. (Universitetets Oldsaksamling, Oslo.)

is: how did the Norsemen go out? We know that they sailed to their new homes in quite large ships, capable of holding a fair number of men, domestic animals and personal equipment. It does not matter whether we call the ships of the emigrants *knorrs* or *longships,* but it is essential to bear in mind two important factors about the 'Viking ship': It was technically on a high level, and it was quite expensive to build. Who had the technical know-how to construct such a ship;* and above all, who had the means for fitting it out?—Continued research on *the Viking ship* and on *Norwegian commerce with other parts of Europe* may throw further light on the background of the Norse expeditions to the West. The suggestions I shall proceed to give are only tentative, as a thorough study of these two subjects is only just developing.

There is a long ship-building tradition behind the Viking

* The reader interested in Viking ship-building should consult T. Sjøvold: *The Vikings Ships (Oslo 1954),* or A.E. Christensen: *Boats of the North (Oslo 1968)*

The Oseberg ship. (Universitetets Oldsaksamling, Oslo.)

ships of the 9th century. We can well understand this when we look at the Oseberg, Tune and Gokstad ships, now in the Viking Ship Museum at Bygdöy, Oslo. Here it is possible to observe the technical improvements in ship-building within a relatively short period by comparing the Oseberg ship built at the beginning of the 9th century with the Gokstad ship which is more than 50 years younger. The general impression we get of the latter is that it is more solidly constructed, as may easily be seen in many details. The keel of the Gokstad ship has a pointed transverse section, and it is cut out in one piece from a choice, straight-grown oak. The same is the case with the Oseberg ship except that its keel does not protrude so much from the hull. Another detail worth noting is the gunwale. It is higher above the water level in the Gokstad than in the Oseberg ship. But both these ships are definitely superior to their predecessors of the 8th and 7th centuries: for instance the Kvalsund ship of

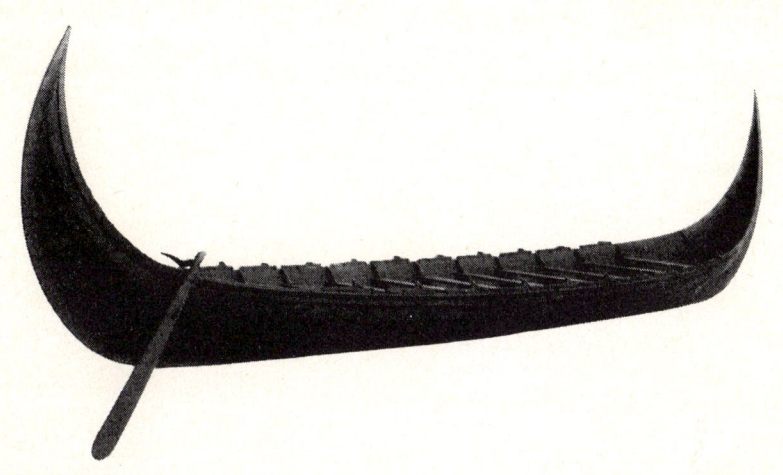

Model of the Kvalsund ship from Sunnmöre, western Norway, (Bergen Sjöfartsmuseum, Bergen.)

northwestern Norway and the bigger Nydam ship of south Jutland. Unlike the Viking ships, these older vessels have no real keel.—Finally we should mention the most important innovation of all: the mast, sail and rigging. In this special field, however, the historian is faced with considerable problems, as no sails and very little of the rigging of the Viking ships have been preserved. Nevertheless it is probably in the sailing ability of the Viking ship that we find one of the main clues to the large-scale maritime invasion of western Europe and the North Atlantic islands. Another important asset of these ships is their shallow draught. The Gokstad ship, for instance, draws only 33.5 inches. Although modern historians hesitate to connect any of the three excavated ships with certain historical individuals in Norwegian history, there can be no doubt as to the place and rank in society of the persons buried in them. The ship-mounds of Gokstad, Tune and Oseberg have been constructed over members of royal or chieftain families.

To what extent did *trade* in general contribute to the prosperity of Norway in the Viking period, and in particular to the economic resources of the shipbuilding aristocracy?

We have already dealt with such sources as the sagas, Ottar's account, the merchant and market laws, all substantiating the existence of a Norwegian domestic and foreign trade during the Viking age. We have also accepted the *coin material* as an indication of trade. In the final pages of this chapter we shall return to this important group of sources and consider the Norwegian coin material in its Scandinavian and European context. We would like to map the chronological trends in the circulation of coins.

The late Danish historian Aksel E. Christensen has given the following approximate figure of Viking-age coins found in Scandinavia (*Vikingetidens Danmark* p. 196, 1969):

Sweden: 100,000 Arabic or Kufic coins, 60,000 of which have been found in Gotland;
35,000 Anglo-Saxon coins (25,000 in Gotland);
75,000 German coins (40,000 in Gotland);
420 Byzantine coins (400 in Gotland);

Denmark: 4,000 Kufic coins, 800 of which have been found in Bornholm;
4,000 Anglo-Saxon coins (3,600 in Bornholm);
9,000 German coins (500 in Bornholm);
46 Byzantine coins (13 in Bornholm);

125,000 of Sweden's foreign coins, 5,000 of Denmark's have been found in the relatively isolated islands of Gotland and Bornholm.

If we turn now to *the Norwegian material* we find that the coin groups are composed as follows: 400 Kufic, 3000 Anglo-Saxon, 3500 German and 26 Byzantine coins. The important question then is: What can the dates of the coins and the dates of the deposits tell about the direction of the flow of coins and about the chronological trends in the material? In Norway it is quite evident that the Kufic coins predominate in the period anterior to 950, while the Anglo-Saxon and German coins have almost a complete monopoly between 950 and 1050. Then at the end of the Viking period the national coinage begins in Norway and the other Scandinavian countries, excluding foreign coins from circulation.

In order to decide the importance of the Oriental silver to the trade of the 9th century, it is also necessary to establish the

The Lummelunda hoard, Gotland (ATA Stockholm, photo Nils Lagergreen 1968).

chronological composition of the 9th and 10th century hoards and finds, both as to dates of issue of the coins and the dates of laying down the deposits. We then get a fairly simple picture for Norway. About two-thirds of the Kufic coins found in Norway were issued by the Samanid dynasty of Transoxania in Central Asia between 895 and 925. A similar concentration is to be found in Sweden and Denmark. In Norway most of the remaining one-third, however, belong to earlier issues by the Abbasids of Baghdad. The greater part of the deposits were made during the 11th century and especially its first half. Thus the flow of Kufic coins was streaming westward in the 9th century, starting like a brook, expanding into a river in the late 9th and the very early 10th century, then drying up in the middle of that century. It was followed by a stream of Anglo-Saxon and German coins in the opposite direction. Trade and war accompanied the diffusion of the Kufic coins in Europe

The Urnes porch from the Urnes stave church, Sogn, western Norway. (Universitetets Oldsaksamling, Oslo.)

from the Russian plains through Scandinavia to the British Isles (where 135 Kufic coins have so far been found, mostly within the Norse sphere of influence). War, Christianization, and the unification of Norway followed in the wake of the Anglo-Saxon pennies.

It does not seem possible at the present stage of research to decide which of these main causes of the Viking expeditions from Norway is the more important. And we should not forget other explanatory elements in the general background, which have only been touched on here—or not dealt with at all. These include improvements in the iron and steel production, which possibly converted it into an industry taking place in certain mountain areas of southern Norway at almost every farm; a political unrest in Norway at the end of the 9th and the first half of the 10th century, causing a certain emigration to Iceland and other islands in the west; an expanding domestic trade, feeding the coastal markets with the commodities of the hinterland; the Viking greed for booty, causing young men by scores to join their chieftains in daring raids against western Europe; the spirit of adventure, probably nourished by the preference for death in battle rather than in bed, an important element in the old pagan religion; and the weakened royal and princely authority in some states of western Europe, the non-existent authority of the state in parts of eastern Europe.

VI. EPILOGUE

In his book *Ancient Emigrants* (1929), the Norwegian archaeologist A. W. Brögger has emphasized two important aspects of the Norse Viking expansion: the exodus as a drain on the population of Norway and the unparalleled cultural effort of the Norsemen during the Viking centuries.—It is Brögger's grand idea that the emigration from Norway in the Viking age might be comparable to that taking place in the 19th and 20th centuries to America. In the course of a century 800,000 persons emigrated out of a population which in 1825 counted one million and in 1929 2.8 millions. It is no doubt a realistic comparison when we take into account the territories settled by the Norsemen in the Viking period: parts of Normandy, Ireland, the Isle of Man, and northwestern England, the Hebrides, Sutherland, Caithness, the Orkneys, Shetland, the Faroes, Iceland and Greenland. Of course, we do not possess any figures, either of the population in Norway in the Viking period or of the number of people in the Norse colonies in the 11th century, but when we bear in mind the relatively dense Norse population in some of these areas (Iceland, the Orkneys, the Isle of Man), Brögger's comparison seems tenable.

His thesis of the early Viking period as a time of cultural splendour, 'a golden age', has gained ascendancy in modern historical writing. The 'Viking achievement' is in the limelight of modern interest. And it seems as if the culture of Scandinavia, not only in the Viking centuries proper (800-1050), but also in the Middle Ages in general, has received the label 'Viking'.

It is essential to bear in mind what changes were caused by an internal Norwegian development, and what were the influences from the outside world which would have some impact on Norse society. Although Norway of the Viking age probably left an important oral literature (later to be recorded in writing), produced such monuments of ship-building technique as the Gokstad, Tune, and Oseberg ships, and such social institutions as the *things,* Norway remained a barbarous country until the introduction of Christian and Latin culture. With Christianity came a certain knowledge of classical culture, of writing, and of social organization based on a centralized pattern. With Christianity came a new ethical code and a new spirit, which implied a death blow to the warlike ideals of the Vikings of the 9th and 10th centuries.

But certain ideals of the Viking age never died and were carried on by later generations of Christianized Norsemen. One of these should not be be left unmentioned:

> 'Wealth dies,
> kinsmen die,
> a man dies likewise himself;
> I know one thing
> that never dies,
> the verdict on each man dead'.
> *(Hávamál*)*

*) Translation by P. Foote & D. M. Wilson: *The Viking Achievement,* p. 432.

LIST OF ADDITIONAL READING

B. Almgren, Ch. Blindheim et alia, *The Viking* (Lond. 1966).
A. Binns, *Viking Voyagers. Then and Now* (Lond. 1980).
M.A.S. Blackburn and D. M. Metcalf, eds., *Viking-Age Coinage in the Northern Lands* (Oxf. 1981).
A Fenton and H. Pálsson, eds., *The Northern and Western Isles in the Viking World* (Edinb. 1984).
P. Foote and D. M. Wilson, *The Viking Achievement* (Lond. 1970).
J. Graham-Campbell, *The Viking World*, (Lond. 1980).
G. Jones, *The Norse Atlantic Saga* (Oxf. 1964).
G. Jones, *A History of the Vikings* (Oxf. 1968).
F. D. Logan, *The Vikings in History* (Lond. 1983)
M. Magnusson, *Vikings!* (Lond. 1980).
D. Ó. Corrain, *Ireland before the Normans* (Dublin 1972).
P. H. Sawyer, *The Age of the Vikings* (Lond. 1971).
P.H. Sawyer, *Kings and Vikings* (Lond. 1982).
J. Simpson, *Everyday Life in the Viking Age* (Lond. 1967).
D.M. Wilson and O. Klindt-Jensen, Viking Art (Lond. 1966).

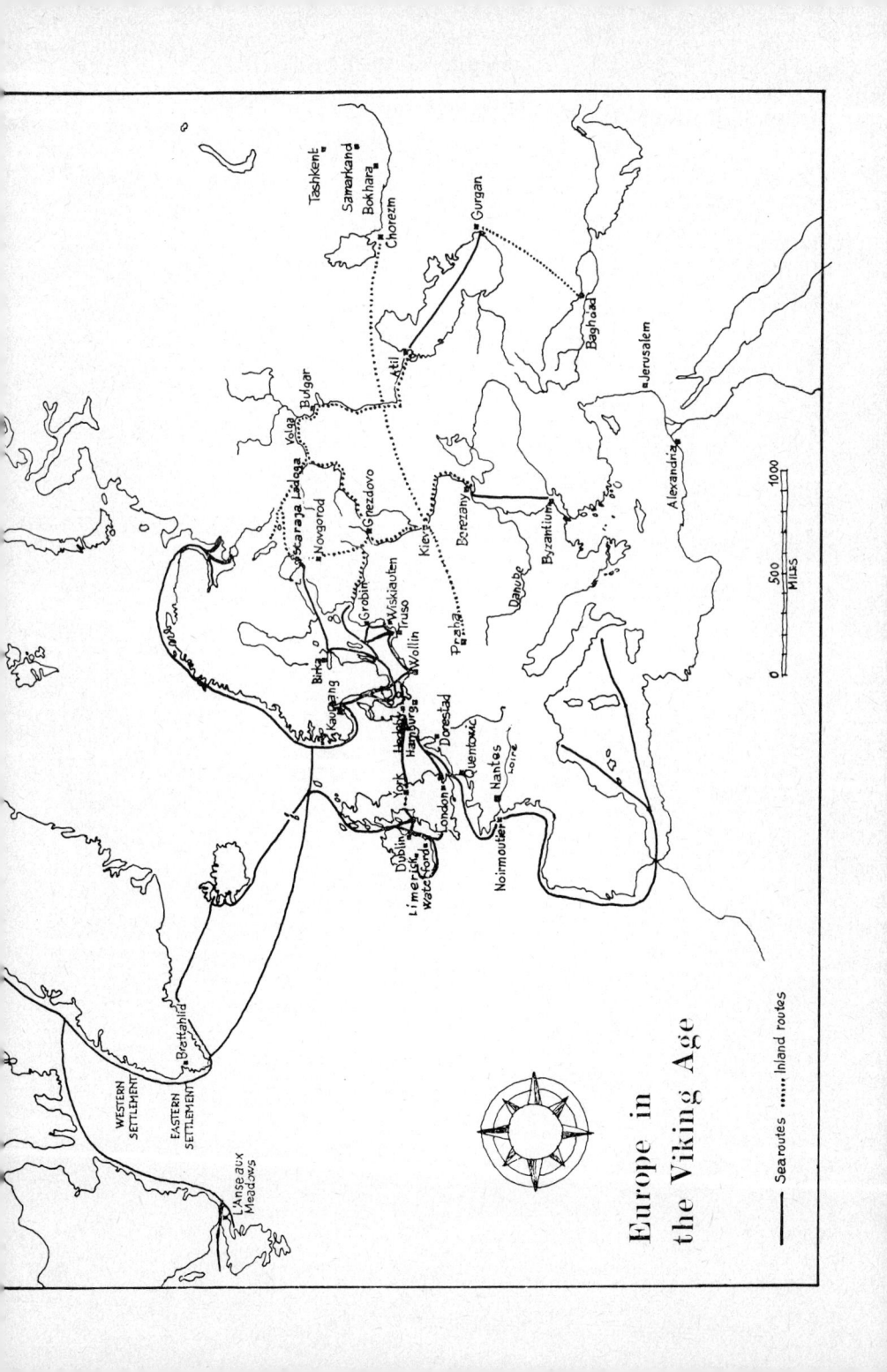

Europe in
the Viking Age

—— Sea routes ······ Inland routes

INDEX

Agriculture, 18, 26, 33, 44—53, 71.
Alstad stone, 13.
Anglo-Saxon Chronicle, 11, 16, 53, 74.
Arabic world, 9, 12. *See also* Coins.
Archaeological studies, 12, 17, 34, 86.
Ari froði, 46, 79.
Arrows, 43—45, 63.
Axes, 22, 39, 40, 42.

Bayeux Tapestry, 39, 45, 59.
Binns, A. L., 75.
Birsay, 70, 71.
Blindheim, C., 30.
Boats, *see* Ship.
Bolin, S., 9, 19, 33, 68.
Bonde, 24, 46. *See also* Agriculture.
Bows, 43—45.
British Isles, 26, 69. *See also* England etc.
Brögger, A. W., 98.

Caithness, 66, 71, 83.
Campaigns of conquest, 9, 14, 72, 74—77, 83, 84, 96—97. *See also* Piratical raids.
Carvings, 14, 60, 61, 96.
Celtic, *see* Irish.
Christianity, *see* Religion.
Churches and church sites, 19, 24, 70, 79, 96.
Clothing, 51—52. *See also* Ornaments.
Coins, 19—21, 30—33, 94—97:
 Anglo-Saxon, 20, 21, 31, 94, 95, 97.
 Byzantine, 21, 94.
 Frankish, 21, 30.
 German, 20, 94, 95.
 Kufic, 20, 21, 30, 31, 32, 94—96.
Crosses, 13, 72, 75.
Cumberland, 75, 76.
Danelaw, 74, 83.
Dublin, 56, 72—73, 76, 83.

Edda, The Poetic, 50, 99.
Ekwall, E., 75.
England, 14, 15, 16, 74—76, 83—84.
Eric Bloodaxe, 36, 64, 76.
Faroes, The, 19, 45, 46, 66, 78, 79, 84.
Fishing, 22, 46, 52, 54, 80.

Fitjar, 36—38.
Food and Drink, 49, 58.
Frankish Empire, 30, 41, 77, 84.

Galteland stone, 14.
Gokstad ship, 48, 91—93.
Grave-finds, 18, 22—24, 26—27, 28, 33, 38, 39, 44, 88. *See also* Ship graves.
Greenland, 10, 17, 66, 79—81, 84.
Gudbrandsdalen, 90.

Hafrsfjord, 28, 37.
Hákon the Good, 36.
Hallingdal, 90.
Harald Fairhair, 28, 30, 58, 62, 69, 76, 78.
Harald Hardradi, 11, 58.
Hebrides 16, 22, 33, 34, 66, 71, 83.
Helmets, 37, 38.
Hirðmenn, 39, 57, 58.
Historia Norwegiae, 70.
Holtan, 31, 34.
House-carls, 57.
Houses, 25—26, 46—49.
Hunting, 44, 46, 52, 54, 80.

Iceland, 10, 19, 31, 45, 46, 58, 66, 79—80, 84, 90.
Ingstad, A. S. and H., 81, 82.
Ireland, 53, 66, 72, 75, 83.
Irish (Celtic) influences, 20, 23, 26, 27, 30, 31, 33, 72, 75.
Iron, Working of, 42, 46, 97.

Jaeren, 20, 26, 27, 34, 45.
Jarlshof, 25—26, 27, 34, 46, 70.

Kaupang; Skiringsal, 28, 30, 34, 54, 56; later Nidaros, 56.
Kings and courts, 56—62.
Kirk Michael, 13.
Knoc-y-Doonee, 22, 33.
Kvalsund ship, 26, 92—93.

Lancashire 75, 76.
Landnámabók, 31, 79.
L'Anse-aux-Meadows, 81, 82.
Laws, legal system, 21, 43, 55, 62—64.

Larvik, 28.
Long-houses, 25, 46, 47.
Long-ships, *see* Ship.

Mail-shirts, 39.
Man, Isle of, 13, 22—23, 33, 34, 66, 71, 83.
Markets in Norway, 30, 31, 54, 56, 97.
Marwick, H., 70.
Møre, 34, 77, 89.
Munch, P. A., 28.

Nantes, 77.
Newfoundland, 17, 81, 82.
Nidaros, 31, 56, 62.
Noirmoutier, 77, 78, 84.
Normandy, 77, 84.
North Norway, 28, 29, 63.
Northumberland, 75, 83.
Northumbria, 74—76.

Olav Haraldsson (the Saint), 40, 55, 60, 62.
Olav Tryggvesson, 40.
Olsen, M., 87.
Orkney, 16, 17, 19, 23, 34, 53, 66, 70, 83, 90.
Ornaments, 18, 20, 23, 24, 26, 27, 28, 33, 34, 61.
Oseberg ship, 60, 61, 63, 92.
Østfold, 21.
Ottar, 28, 54.

Personal names, 12, 16, 17.
Petersen, J., 41.
Pierowall, 23—25, 34, 70, 71.
Piratical raids, 10, 12, 18, 27, 34, 53, 57, 66, 72, 97.
Place-names, 12, 15—17, 71, 73—76, 86—90.
Population growth, 9, 86, 87, 89, 90, 98.

Ragnvald, Earl, 24.
Religion: pagan, 61, 62, 75, 97; Christian, 10, 15, 18, 19, 62, 66, 99.
Rogaland, 18, 21, 32, 89.
Rollo, 77, 84.
Runic inscriptions, 12, 13—15, 72.
Russia, Norse contacts with, 12, 13, 31, 55, 96.
Rygh, O., 87.

Sagas, 21, 40, 42, 49, 81:
    Egils, 64—66.

Faereyinga, 78.
Heimskringla, 36, 37, 40, 54, 57.
Orkneyinga, 24, 53, 70.
Sawyer, P. H., 16, 74.
Scotland, 16, 19, 22—24, 54. *See also* Hebrides, etc.
Settlement: expansion within Norway, 86—90; expansion overseas, 69—85; selection of sites, 18—19, 71—73, 75, 77.
Shetland, 24—26, 34, 46, 66, 70, 83, 90.
Shields, 39.
Ship: of war, 37, 38, 56, 64, 66; of commerce, 54, 91. *See also* ships named.
Ship- and boat-graves, 22, 24, 30, 33, 60—61, 93.
Ship-building, 66—67, 79, 91—93, 98.
Skaldic poems, 14, 36, 42, 58, 64.
Skiringsal, *see* Kaupang.
Snorre Sturlason. 14, 36, 40.
Sognefjord, 28, 34, 88, 89.
Spears, 39—42.
Stavanger, 26.
Steinkjer, 31.
Sumburgh Voe, 24—26.
Swords, 22, 30, 39, 41—43.

Tapestry, 61, 63. *See also* Bayeux Tapestry.
Thing, 39, 62—67, 99.
Thralls, 50, 51, 57.
Trade: Norwegian internal, 54, 56, 87, 97; Norwegian oversea, 30, 31, 34, 53—56, 72, 73, 75, 83—84, 87, 94—97; Scandinavian, 9—10, 14, 20, 68, 77, 94.
Trøndelag, 21, 28, 31, 34, 45, 63, 88—90.
Trondheim, *see* Nidaros.
Tune ship, 92.

Valdres, 90.
Valtos, 22, 33.
Vestfold, 18, 28, 32, 34, 60, 77.
Viking, 26, 35—36, 53, 98.
Vinland, 10, 81.

Wales, South, 75, 84.
Weapons and Armour, 37—44. *See also* Axe, etc.
Westmorland, 75, 76.

York, Yorkshire, 74, 75.